POLEMIC CHAT

BY

EDMUND M. DUNNE

BISHOP OF PEORIA

ST. LOUIS, MO., 1912
Published by B. Herder
17 South Broadway

Freiburg (Baden) Germany	68, Great Russell Str. London, W. C.

COPYRIGHT, 1912, BY JOSEPH GUMMERSBACH

FOREWORD

As indicated by the title, this brochure is professedly polemic. Its aim is the refutation of a few popular fallacies regarding religious truth. Most of the chapters have already appeared in the Peoria Cathedral Calendar. The dialogue, while imaginary in spots, is largely the reproduction of conversations that actually occurred between individuals whose names have been thinly disguised or entirely changed so as to avoid embarrassment.

We have taken the liberty of placing Fr. Michaels in charge of St. Anne's parish, Mackinac, with due apologies to the esteemed rector of that congregation. Our polemist might have been assigned just as easily to a pastorate in Madagascar, Capri or Timbuctoo; but then he would be too far away to awaken interest. The fact is that with our strong predilection for that fascinating emerald gem in a setting of turquoise water, Mackinac Island, on which we spent many a pleasant vacation, we simply could not resist domiciling him there and thus giving a local tinge to our narrative.

The experiences of Fr. Michaels are by no means unique. Far more thrilling incidents happen, we presume, to the average priest in the ordinary routine of his daily life.

If the perusal of these pages be instrumental in bringing a single stray sheep into the one true fold and to the practice of the one true religion, we shall feel amply compensated.

The Author.

CONTENTS

CHAPTER		PAGE
I	Participation in False Worship	1
II	Evil of Mixed Marriages	7
III	Divorce	15
IV	A Prospective Convert	20
V	Religious Indifference	25
VI	One True Religion	31
VII	Nuptial Mass	35
VIII	Catholic Education	41
IX	Secret Societies	46
X	Index of Prohibited Books	51
XI	Existence of God	56
XII	The Most Holy Trinity	61
XIII	Divinity of Christ	66
XIV	The Redemption	71
XV	The Blessed Virgin	75
XVI	Fallacy of Christian Science	80
XVII	Confession	85
XVIII	The Holy Eucharist	90
XIX	Symbolism of Vestments and Ceremonies	95
XX	Cremation	100
XXI	Predestination	106
XXII	Existence of Hell	110
XXIII	Capital Punishment	114
XXIV	Necessity of Religion	118
XXV	Gambling	122
XXVI	Dancing	127
XXVII	The Theatre	131
XXVIII	Woman Suffrage	135
XXIX	Catholic Priesthood	140
XXX	A Catholic (?) Socialist	144
XXXI	Vocation	149

POLEMIC CHAT

CHAPTER I

PARTICIPATION IN FALSE WORSHIP

'Twas a glorious summer morning on the Island of Mackinac. Not a cloud in the sky, nor scarcely a ripple on the broad expanse of water, which was dotted here and there with small sailing craft evidently marooned, owing to the stillness of the atmosphere. Mr. Grebma and his guests were enjoying their matutinal smoke on the veranda of his comfortable summer cottage situated on a bluff overlooking the straits. The Chicago papers, which always came a day late, had been read and cast aside. The company had discussed exhaustively pro and con the colossal fine imposed upon the Standard Oil Trust, and the conversation began to lag. The silence was broken by the occasional warble of an oriole in a neighboring tree or by the buzz of a humming bird that flitted about the flower baskets suspended from the ceiling of the veranda.

While the gaze of the smokers wandered listlessly from the boats lying motionless, like so many aquatic fowl upon the water's surface, to the greedy robins pulling worms from the green lawn that stretched like an emerald Wilton carpet from the house to the roadside, their attention was suddenly aroused by the approach of Father Michaels, the local pastor. He waved his hand in greeting to the gentlemen on the porch. Mr. Grebma returned the salutation, shouting at the same time: "Good morning, Father! What's your hurry? Won't you come up and join us?"

The priest accepted the proffered invitation; he was always a welcome visitor at the Grebma cottage. For some unaccountable reason his presence seemed invariably to turn the theme of conversation to religious topics. "We had quite a theological discussion at the breakfast table this morning," said Mr. Grebma, "and we should like very much to have you throw a little light on the subject."

"Well, what is the subject under discussion?" asked the clergyman, helping himself to a perfecto from a box that lay alluringly open on the table and settling himself down in a cozy rocker.

"Why, the subject is Uncle Joe Cannon," said Mr. Grebma. "I suppose you know that he will be in town to-night?"

"Yes," replied the priest, "I heard some persons talking about him this morning at the postoffice when I dropped in there to get my mail."

"We have been debating," continued Mr. Grebma, "about the propriety of our going to hear him speak. He is a national character and mentioned as a presidential possibility. I am very curious to see him. People say that he looks exactly like the pictures of him in the newspapers. He must be a pretty shrewd and able fellow to be Speaker of the House."

"Where is he going to speak?" asked the priest.

"In the town hall," replied Mr. Grebma. "The women folks claim that I must not go, because he intends to speak for the benefit of the little Protestant church. Of course you will agree with them. My candid opinion is that you all are too narrow-gauged in such things. What harm can there be in helping those people to maintain their church? Isn't it better to aid them in keeping the church they have than to allow them to be without one? You will say that for me it would be participation in a false worship; but as the old darkey sagely remarked: 'De sinfulness ob sin am pendin' on de spirit which you goes and does it in.' I simply want to see and hear Uncle Joe. That is the purpose of my going. The fact that a collection will be taken up for the benefit of the Protestant church doesn't concern me. Of course I will be obliged to give something in order not to appear mean."

"Why, certainly," interposed Judge McIlhon. "I fail to see anything wrong in that. In our town the Methodists,

Baptists and Presbyterians come around to my office regularly for a subscription whenever there is anything going on in their churches, and I always write them out a check. There is no escape. They do the same for us. Look at Bishop So-and-So; didn't he get nearly half a million from a non-Catholic for his seminary? Why, it isn't so very long ago that the newspapers had a report of this same prelate making a donation to the Y. M. C. A."

"Gentlemen," said the priest, "while I do not assert that it would be wrong for you to attend this lecture, my advice is to remain at home. Charity obliges us to love all men irrespective of creed, color or nationality. We hate false principles, but not the persons holding them. The fact of their helping us to support the one true church is certainly no reason why we should help them to maintain a false one. You cannot place truth and error upon an equal footing. Please answer me this question: 'Do you believe the Catholic Church to be the only true one established by Christ?'"

"We do believe," they replied, in unison that reminded him of a class of first communicants renewing their baptismal vows.

"And that all other churches outside the true one are false?"

"We do believe," they answered.

"Then," added the priest, "you cannot help perceiving the fallacy of your assertion that it is better to help them support their false church than to have none at all. As well might you say that it is better to help a man to keep at least counterfeit money than allow him to go with his pockets empty. Nothing is easier than to enunciate moral principles regarding formal and material co-operation in a false worship. But the practical application of these principles is not so easy. It is often difficult to determine whether the co-operation be really formal or only material; even in the latter case it does not follow that material co-operation is always permissible. There must be a just and sufficient motive which can only be decided in each individual case according to the rules of prudence and common sense. Architects, for example, are justified in drawing plans, likewise contractors and laborers in executing the same in the construction of synagogues and heretical temples. Their co-operation is not formal, but material, and there is besides the just and urgent motive of earning an honest living. Now in the case of your attending to-night's lecture for the benefit of the Protestant church, your co-operation would be only material. But where is the just and urgent motive for your attendance? Is it lest your absence might hurt you socially or financially? You will suffer no damage by remaining away. Your sole motive is to satisfy your curiosity which may be amply gratified when you return to Chicago or visit Washington. Of course I realize how embarrassing it must be on certain occasions for business and professional men, whom commercial and social interests bring in daily contact with non-Catholics. It is sometimes practically impossible to refuse them when they solicit funds for their churches. I think it would be well to tell them plainly: ' Gentlemen, my conscience forbids me to contribute to the support of a denomination which I sincerely believe to be false. To show that there is no ill feeling, here is a donation for your orphans, for your hospital or for the poor of your congregation.' This will preclude all possibility of being considered mean, and at the same time elicit admiration for the courage of your religious convictions. It is related of Archbishop Hughes that he was once asked to contribute to the erection of a new Protestant church by certain parties to whom he felt under special obligations. He told the solicitors that he could not contribute to the erection of a Protestant church, but would gladly give a donation to pull down the old one. His action was solely a manifestation of good will and could in no wise be interpreted as an endorsement of heresy.

" A similar explanation may no doubt be found in regard to the prelate contributing to the Y. M. C. A. We should, however, keep in mind that according to its constitution, no Catholic is eligible to any office in that organization. The late Count Creighton of Omaha stopped his contributions to it rather abruptly when he became aware of this discriminating clause. This feature alone, apart from its underhand proselytizing proclivities, ought to be sufficient reason for us to think twice before consenting to be advertised as patrons of such an institution. We certainly have ample opportunity to exercise charity a little nearer home."

"Father," asked the Judge, "what about Catholics attending marriages, baptisms, sermons and funerals in Protestant churches? Did you notice the fuss a western bishop made over a Catholic lady acting as bridesmaid at the wedding of a divorced man? Why, the papers reported that he threatened to excommunicate any Catholic attending the ceremony! Don't you think that he was a little too drastic and intolerant?"

"No," said Father Michaels, "I think that the bishop was perfectly justified in his action. What business could self-respecting Catholics possibly have at such a scandalous performance? Their presence would be easily interpreted not only as condoning, but as sanctioning legalized adultery. In the first place, Catholics are never allowed to assist at heretical weddings or baptisms in the capacity of bridesmaids or sponsors, as the Church has more than once expressly declared. Sermons of heretics should be also avoided. 'A man that is a heretic,' says Paul, 'after the first and second admonition avoid. Shun profane and vain babblings, for they grow much towards ungodliness. And their speech spreadeth like a canker of whom are Hymeneus and Philetus. He that loveth the danger shall perish therein.' The custom of inviting heretics and infidels to address Catholic assemblies on ethical subjects is even more reprehensible. Such individuals are certainly not qualified to teach us anything on religious topics. In regard to funerals, it may be allowed to attend them simply as an act of friendship and courtesy, provided, of course, you take no part whatever in the religious service, provided there be neither occasion of scandal nor danger of perversion, and above all that there really exists an urgent reason for being present at such functions. In all cases of this kind it is best to seek advice beforehand from the ecclesiastical authorities, since it was for the purpose of guiding the faithful in their spiritual difficulties that our Lord appointed bishops and pastors over His Church. Well, gentlemen, I hate to tear myself away, but duty calls. A person telephoned me from the town that he desired to have an interview with me at eleven o'clock and I must not disappoint him. Good bye."

CHAPTER II

EVIL OF MIXED MARRIAGES

On his way home Fr. Michaels stopped at the postoffice for his mail. As he sauntered along the board walk, lining the shore, he perused the few letters he had received. One of them was from his bishop, allowing him to be away from his parish over Sunday, provided he found a priest to take his place during his absence. The others were stereotyped communications from stock brokers, confidentially promising to let him in on the ground floor of a get-rich-quick scheme that would net him about 15 per cent. The good father was better versed in polemics than finance, and the fascinating vision of a new pipe organ being installed in his church flashed momentarily across his mind. It was succeeded by the melancholy recollection of an unprofitable investment which, a year or so after his ordination, he had persuaded an indulgent parent to make for him. He had learned through painful experience that in the marts of this cruel world, we cannot get something for nothing. "Served me right," he muttered. "*Ne sutor supra crepidam.*"[1] If these alluring investments were really what their promoters represent, the shrewd speculators always on the alert for a good thing would not allow a dollar of the stock to escape. He therefore consigned the advertising baits to the tender mercy of the waves, where the unsuspecting fishes might nibble at them if they chose.

When he finally reached the parish rectory, he found a young man in the parlor. "Good morning, Father," said the visitor, rising and at the same time proffering his card. "My name is George Paxton, and I telephoned you from the Island House. I want to arrange with you about a marriage."

"This is rather sudden, Mr. Paxton," said the priest, smiling

[1] Let the cobbler stick to his last.

and glancing at the inscription on the card. "I see you are from Chicago. And the young lady?"

"Her home is also in Chicago, but just now she is stopping with friends over at the East End. She isn't a Catholic. I am having a couple of weeks vacation and arrived here yesterday on the *Northland* from Duluth. We happened to meet yesterday on the dock by the merest accident. She came down to see a few friends leave on the Detroit boat. We have been keeping company nearly two years. In fact, we are engaged and concluded last evening that it would be nice to be married quietly up here."

"It would be nice," said Fr. Michaels, "if you had a dispensation from your bishop and a letter from your pastor authorizing me to marry you."

"Well, Father," said Mr. Paxton, "can't you telegraph for the dispensation? I will stand the expense."

"Your pastor is really the one to apply for the dispensation and to certify that you are free to marry. Rome has more than once reproved the telegraphic mode of granting dispensations. We must observe the canonical formalities."

"And what are they?" anxiously inquired Mr. Paxton.

"Please take a seat," said Fr. Michaels, "and we will talk it over. You say that you are already engaged to this young lady?"

"Yes, Father."

"Was she ever baptized in any church?"

"Well, you have me there, Father," said Mr. Paxton. "I really don't know. Does it make any material difference?"

"Enough," replied Fr. Michaels, "to affect the validity of the dispensation. If not baptized, the marriage impediment is called disparity of cult. If she be really baptized, then you must ask for a dispensation from the impediment of mixed religion. For aught I know, she may be a Jewess, and in that case the petition must be made simply for a dispensation between a Catholic and a Jewess. Our bishops are not inclined to grant a dispensation for these Hebrew alliances, which are usually followed by a civil divorce. While the Catholic is forbidden under pain of excommunication to remarry during the lifetime of the divorced Jewish consort, the latter encounters no obstacle on the part of the synagogue to enter second nuptials. Are your parents living?"

"My mother is living and I reside with her. My father died when I was about nine years old."

"Does she know of your engagement to this young lady?" asked Fr. Michaels.

"N-no," stammered the young man, "I can't say that she does; but I rather think she suspects it."

"Suspects it!" echoed the priest. "Have you decided this most important affair without taking her into consultation?"

"It looks that way," replied Mr. Paxton with a sickly smile. "Asking mother," he continued, "is a little bit old fashioned. You see, Father, I am no spring chicken. In fact, I am going on thirty years of age. Who has a better right to decide this most important affair than the person it chiefly concerns? Of course I intended to tell her."

"You certainly are old enough," said Fr. Michaels, "to display a little more filial deference to your mother, as well as a little more prudence and judgment in a matter of such vital importance. Who, in your candid opinion, is more deeply interested in your welfare — she who brought you into existence and has known you intimately before you even knew yourself, or this lady, whose chance acquaintance you made a few years ago, who after a while may tire of you, seek a divorce and pick up with someone else?"

"Father," said Mr. Paxton, "this young lady is very favorably disposed. More than once she has intimated her willingness to comply with all the conditions of the Church."

"Very obliging," mused the priest. "No doubt she would as readily comply with all the conditions of the synagogue, in case that you happened to be a Jew."

"Well, Father," said Mr. Paxton with some animation, "I happen to be a Catholic instead of a Jew. I'm a traveling man and must admit that I have been a good deal of a sport. Many a hard earned dollar I've lost in poker and on the ponies. My batting average has also been pretty strong. But I've cut it all out and intend to settle down. I might run off to a justice or a preacher and get married, but that would break my mother's heart and God knows I've caused her trouble enough. As a Catholic, I wish to know what is necessary to obtain the dispensation." A stray tear trickled down his cheek as he finished.

"Are you a professional?" asked Fr. Michaels.

"Professional what?" inquired Mr. Paxton with a look of bewilderment.

"Why, a professional ball player," replied Fr. Michaels. "You alluded to your strong batting average. I was quite an enthusiast of the game in my college days."

"Oh," ejaculated Mr. Paxton, "I simply meant hitting the bottle. Kindly tell me how I can get the dispensation."

"My dear friend," said Fr. Michaels, "quite a number of things are necessary for that dispensation. First of all, the lady must sign an agreement that she will never interfere with you in the practice of your religion; that offspring of both sexes shall be brought up in the Catholic Faith; that no other ceremony but the one performed by the priest shall take place. Not only should the danger of your drifting away from the church be remote, but you must do all in your power to bring about her conversion. According to a recent decree a dispensation granted from the impediment disparity of cult *without* a promise regarding these conditions is null, and in each case the nullity of the marriage can be declared by the bishop himself without having recourse to the Holy See. All these requirements are specifically stated in the Apostolic Faculties empowering bishops to grant such dispensations. Besides these written promises, there must be a grave canonical reason without which neither the bishop nor anyone delegated by him can validly dispense. If the petitioners be not poverty stricken, a nominal alms is exacted and devoted to some charitable work at the bishop's discretion."

"What would be regarded as a grave canonical reason for granting the dispensation?" asked Mr. Paxton.

"A well-founded prospect of converting the non-Catholic,"

replied Fr. Michaels. "In the case of a Catholic girl, who is not a widow, the fact of her being 24 years of age. It might be her only opportunity for a suitable match. A dispensation might be granted in order to prevent week-kneed Catholics from marrying sacrilegiously outside the Church and living in sin."

"Why, Father, from your talk," exclaimed Mr. Paxton, "one would infer that the Church doesn't approve of mixed marriages. Yet she grants dispensations for them every day."

"Rest assured," said Fr. Michaels, "that she does not approve of them. Whenever she allows her children to marry a person outside her communion, the dispensation should not be regarded as a tacit approval or encouragement of such a union, but merely as a toleration or selection of the lesser of two evils. If there be anything contrary to the spirit of true religion, it is mixed marriages. Even granting that the promises have been sincerely made, what assurance is there that they will be faithfully kept? There is no relationship more intimate than that of man and wife. But what unity of feeling and sentiment can exist between hearts that hold contrary religious convictions? Habits, customs and relationships constantly clash and the opposing religious views of the married couple are a permanent source of domestic strife. The non-Catholic wife promises not to interfere with the Catholic husband in the practice of his religion. But very likely she and her relatives have been taught to regard the Pope as anti-Christ, the priests as wolves in sheep's clothing, the veneration of the Saints and devotion to the Holy Eucharist as idolatry, confession a human invention, fasting and abstinence as rank superstition! Will they allow the children to be inoculated with such awful practices? Not if they can help it. I once knew a fine Catholic young man who married a highly respected lady not of his faith. They have a son aged 14 who has never been baptized. Of course some of these unions may result in the sincere conversion of the non-Catholic and the Christian education of the children. But for such an exceptionally fortunate mixed marriage, a score of unhappy ones may be easily adduced as horrible examples. For this reason they were positively forbidden to the ancient Jews and emphatically discouraged among Christians."

"I never heard of mixed marriages among the ancient Jews," said Mr. Paxton.

"Well, just listen to this," said Fr. Michaels, picking up a Bible that lay on the center table and turning to Genesis VI: "The sons of God seeing the daughters of men that they were fair, took to themselves wives of all which they chose."

"Why are they called the sons of God?" asked the young man.

"Did you never read," said Fr. Michaels, "the words of St. John's gospel recited at the end of Mass — 'But as many as received him, He gave them power to be made the sons of God?' The descendants of Seth and Enos on account of their religion and piety are called sons of God. They remained good until they married the ungodly race of Cain, styled on account of their iniquity the sons of men. The unhappy consequence of their intermarriage is clearly indicated in verse 17: 'Behold I will bring the waters of a great flood upon the earth to destroy all flesh.' This ought to render Christians most circumspect in their marriages. They should never be influenced in the choice of a life partner by wealth or passion to the prejudice of virtue or religion. Jacob following the advice of his worthy parents went to the country of his ancestors to seek in marriage the hand of Rachel and thus became the father of God's chosen people. By ignoring the counsel of your mother, you evidently wish to follow the pernicious example of Esau, who selected a heathen wife, thus bringing untold grief to his parents.

"In Deuteronomy VI, we see how the people of Israel are commanded to have no fellowship with the pagan Chanaanites. 'Neither shalt thou make marriage with them. Thou shalt not give thy daughter to his son, nor take his daughter for thy son. For she will turn away thy son from following me that he may rather serve strange gods, and the wrath of the Lord will be kindled and will quickly destroy thee.'"

"But don't you think, Father," said Mr. Paxton, "that we enjoy greater freedom in this respect under the New Law?"

"St. Paul doesn't think so," replied Fr. Michaels. "Read what he says in II Cor. VI, 14, 15."

The young man turned to the passage indicated and read aloud: "Bear not the yoke with unbelievers. For what participation hath justice with injustice? Or what fellowship hath light with darkness? And what concord hath Christ with Belial? Or what part hath the faithful with the unbeliever? What's the answer?" asked Mr. Paxton.

"A decidedly negative answer," replied the priest solemnly. "No participation, no fellowship, no part. Speaking of the widow's freedom to marry after her husband's death, the apostle says in I Cor. VII: 'Let her marry to whom she will, only in the Lord.' The meaning is — Let her get married in the Church; not to a pagan, Jew, infidel or heretic, but to a Christian. Councils and Pontiffs are unanimous in discouraging these unfortunate alliances. The Church's attitude is clearly manifested in the conspicuous absence of religious ceremonies at their celebration. Nuptial Mass and blessing are omitted. In fact, they cannot take place in the church or in any part of it. Bishops generally decline to officiate, in deference to the wishes of the Sovereign Pontiff. The priest standing before the couple merely as a witness is forbidden by the Roman Ritual to wear stole or other sacred vestment."

"But why should the Church be so intolerant," asked Mr. Paxton, "especially here in America, where we come in daily contact with heretics, Jews and infidels?"

"My dear sir," replied Fr. Michaels, "the child's catechism answers your question. The Church forbids the marriage of Catholics with persons having a different religion or no religion at all, because such marriages generally lead to indifference, loss of faith and to the neglect of the religious education of the children."

"Well, Father," said Mr. Paxton, looking at his watch, "I did not realize that it was so late — a quarter of one. I want to thank you for the trouble you have taken with me. There are a few more things I would like to know. When may I impose again on your time?"

"To-morrow morning about 11 o'clock," replied Fr. Michaels. "As to the alleged imposition, put that out of your head. My time could not be better employed. If I succeed in dissuading you from entering upon an alliance which means inevitable misery, I shall feel amply compensated."

CHAPTER III

DIVORCE

"I am glad to see you so punctual," said Fr. Michaels, as he ushered Mr. Paxton into his library the next morning.

"Oh, I always try to keep an appointment," replied the latter. "Father," he continued, "I want to be perfectly frank. Open confession, they say, is good for the soul. The young lady to whom I am engaged was married before."

"You don't tell me!" exclaimed Fr. Michaels, staring in blank amazement at his visitor.

"Yes," said Mr. Paxton, with his gaze fixed upon the floor. "She was married to a worthless, drunken fellow, who, on several occasions, threatened to kill her. He finally left her and went out west to Arizona. She obtained a divorce from him on the grounds of cruelty and desertion. I don't consider that any real marriage. Of course as a general rule the Catholic Church never grants a divorce. My employer has made rules which I break occasionally for good reasons and he doesn't upbraid me. Why can't the Church do the same?"

"Nothing can solve the bond of a consummated Christian marriage," said Fr. Michaels, "but the death of either husband or wife."

"But why," asked Mr. Paxton, "were the patriarchs and prophets allowed to have several wives?"

"When man's life had been shortened," said Fr. Michaels, "God permitted simultaneous polygamy, in order that His chosen people might be multiplied. He also permitted divorce. But His only begotten Son restored marriage to its original unity and indissolubility. Listen to this," he continued, opening the Bible at St. Mark's gospel, X, 2-12: 'The Pharisees coming to him asked him: Is it lawful for a man to put away his wife? tempting him. But he answering, saith to them: What did Moses command you? Who said: Moses permitted to write a bill of divorce, and to put her away. To whom Jesus answering, said: Because of the hardness of your heart he wrote you that precept. But from the beginning of the creation, God made them male and female. For this cause a man shall leave his father and mother, and shall cleave to his wife. And they two shall be in one flesh. What therefore God hath joined together, let no man put asunder. And in the house again his disciples asked him concerning the same thing. And he saith to them: Whosoever shall put away his wife, and marry another, committeth adultery against her. And if the wife put away her husband, and be married to another, she committeth adultery.' 'To them that are married, not I, but the Lord commandeth,' says St. Paul, I Cor. VII, 'that the wife depart not from her husband. And if she depart, that she remain unmarried, or be reconciled to her husband.' The marriage between infidels, i. e., both unbaptized, may be dissolved in favor of one converted to Christianity, if the unconverted spouse refuses to live peacefully and without contumely to the Creator with the baptized consort. 'If the unbeliever depart, let him depart,' says St. Paul. 'For a brother or sister is not under servitude in such cases. But God hath called us in peace.' The non-consummated marriage of baptized persons may also be dissolved by the solemn profession of one of the parties in a religious order, or by papal dispensation. Sometimes a separation from bed and board may be permitted without the dissolution of the marriage bond, either by mutual consent, or on account of misconduct."

"But isn't marriage a contract just like any other? Why shouldn't it be regulated by the State?" exclaimed Mr. Paxton.

"By no means," replied Fr. Michaels. "As to origin, purpose, rights and duties, marriage differs essentially from all other contracts. The latter regard material, external objects and may be rescinded by mutual consent of the contracting parties. Marriage, being purely domestic and pertaining essentially to the individual, lays the foundation of families on which rests the State. What right has the State to undermine the family? Our Lord raised Christian marriage to the dignity of a Sacrament, thereby placing it among the holiest of religious institutions. By making it a representation of His own union with the Church, it became an outward sign of inward grace. 'The husband,' says St. Paul, 'is the head of the wife, as Christ is the head of the Church.' Therefore, as the Church is subject to Christ, so also let the wives be to their husbands in all things. Husbands, love your wives, as Christ also loved the Church, and delivered Himself up for it. Now marriage could not represent the union of Christ with His Church, and impose special duties on the married couple, unless it also gave them grace to fulfill these duties. Since, therefore, Christ made Christian marriage a sign of His union with the Church, like the other Sacraments, it must be a sign instituted by Christ and productive of grace. Hence the Apostle calls it a 'great Sacrament' (or mystery), 'in Christ and in the Church.' What right then has the State to meddle with it any more than with the other Sacraments? What judge can rightfully declare a valid Christian marriage null and void, any more than he can nullify baptism, confirmation or holy orders? He might just as well try to invalidate the words of consecration or the absolution of the priest. The indissolubility of Christian marriage is not the result of human, but of divine legislation. 'What God hath joined together, let no man put asunder.' Adhering to this principle the Church permitted the apostasy of England rather than grant a decree of nullity to its lustful monarch Henry VIII. For grave reasons Church authority may dispense you from hearing Mass, fasting, abstaining or from other regulations which itself has made. Under no circumstances, however, can priest, prelate or pope dissolve the bond of a consummated Christian marriage any more than they can grant permission to blaspheme, dishonor parents, commit adultery, slander or calumniate. Why? Because such things are forbidden by divine law from which no human authority can dispense."

"Has the State, then, no right to enact laws regarding the marriage of her citizens?" asked Mr. Paxton.

"The State has no right to legalize adultery," replied Fr. Michaels. "It cannot dissolve a valid marriage. While it may legislate regarding the amount of dowry, inheritance, legal obligations of husband and wife, in a word, concerning the civil effects of the marriage contract, the Church alone has the right to make laws regarding the Sacrament of marriage. Catholics are not allowed to apply for a civil divorce without obtaining permission from their bishop beforehand. He will never grant it unless for grave reasons, as e. g. in order to safeguard property rights, to obtain custody of children and protect them from the baneful influence of a worthless parent. If the purpose of the petitioners is to obtain freedom from a valid marriage in order to remarry, they will approach him in vain. Any Catholic man or woman attempting to enter nuptials after having obtained a civil divorce, is debarred from the Sacraments."

"Well, I know of divorced persons, who were remarried by a Catholic priest," exclaimed Mr. Paxton with an air of triumph.

"So do I," replied Fr. Michaels. "And in each case the first marriage was null and void on account of some impediment. People may sometimes go through the marriage ceremony in good faith without being married at all by reason of some circumstance vitiating the marriage contract. To avoid such occurrences the Council of Trent decreed that the names of persons to be married should be published at the principal Mass in the parish church on three Sundays or holidays preceding the marriage. When persons come to arrange for a wedding, they ought to reveal every detail that might invalidate or render their union illicit. But it is usually like pulling teeth to extract the necessary information from them. Yesterday you didn't know whether this lady had ever been baptized. To-day you tell me that she has been divorced from her husband."

"Well, what do you advise me to do?" asked Mr. Paxton in a tone of despair.

"My disinterested advice," replied Fr. Michaels, "is to forget the lady in question. The best way to accomplish this is to avoid meeting or corresponding with her. After you have succeeded in eliminating her from your mind and heart, you can direct your attention to some damsel within the fold not already encumbered with a husband."

"But I have already promised her. How can I break my word?"

"My dear friend," replied Fr. Michaels, "you have no right to promise what your conscience forbids you to do. Supposing that you promised under oath to kill a man, or to burn your neighbor's house? You would certainly commit a grievous sin in making such a promise, and a still more heinous crime in keeping it. It is the same with your engagement to a divorced woman. An oath can never be the bond of iniquity."

CHAPTER IV

A PROSPECTIVE CONVERT

The attention of Fr. Michaels and his visitor was attracted by a phaeton halting before the rectory. "Why, there is the young lady herself," exclaimed Mr. Paxton, at the same time nodding to her through the open window.

"How long do you intend to remain there?" she asked, twirling her parasol.

"Not very long," replied Mr. Paxton. "Please come in a moment; I want you to meet Fr. Michaels. Allow me to present Miss Isabel Seymour," he said, as the young lady entered the parlor. "Very glad to meet you," said Fr. Michaels, slightly coloring.

He was taken by surprise to encounter the individual who had figured so prominently in their conversation. Mr. Paxton enjoyed the priest's embarrassment and remarked facetiously: "Fr. Michaels has been saying some hard things against mixed marriages and divorces."

"Quite true," said Fr. Michaels, regaining his composure. "I have been calling Mr. Paxton's attention to a few Biblical passages on the subject."

"St. Paul, I fancy, is not very much in favor of them," ventured the young lady. "Still," she continued, "if he knew my case, he would readily admit that I have been more sinned against than sinning. Do you think, Father, that he would compel me to live with a human brute who threatened to kill me?"

"Hardly," replied Fr. Michaels.

"Well, that is what John Betruger, my husband, tried to do," said the young woman, as the tears welled in her eyes at the thought of it. "When under the influence of liquor he was capable of anything. In self-protection I procured a divorce from him on the grounds of cruelty and non-support. I have heard and read a good deal about Catholic doctrine and often wished to join the Church. But of course that is impossible for a divorcee."

"The mere fact of your being divorced," said Fr. Michaels, "is no hindrance to your entering the Church. There is joy before the angels in heaven over one sinner doing penance more than over ninety-nine just that need not penance. Our Lord came to save the lost sheep of Israel. Think of the mercy He displayed towards Mary Magdalen and the woman accused by the Pharisees. The greatest reprobate is most cordially welcomed into the Catholic fold provided he be willing to believe and practice what the Church believes and teaches."

"Oh, Father," exclaimed the lady, her face crimsoning, "I certainly am not as wicked as you imagine. What would I have to do in order to become a Catholic?"

"Pardon me," said Fr. Michaels, "but are you not more deeply interested in matrimony than in baptism?"

"Well, I am equally interested in both," she replied, somewhat nettled. "I shall never marry Mr. Paxton without the sanction of his church. Persons familiar with my case have assured me that if it were properly presented before the bishop, I would obtain a favorable decision. The trouble is that no priest to whom I have ever broached the subject cares to bother with it. Doesn't the Church concern herself at all about the marriages of Protestants?"

"The marriage of baptized Protestants," said Fr. Michaels, "is a sacrament and therefore subject to the Church's jurisdiction. She has never exempted heretics from any of her marriage laws, unless perhaps the one of clandestinity. She regards the marriage of a baptized Protestant with an unbaptized person as invalid owing to the impediment of disparity of cult."

"But Father," asked Miss Seymour, "what about the case in which neither husband nor wife is baptized?"

"Such marriages not being a sacrament," replied Fr. Michaels, "the Church has no jurisdiction over them. Jews and infidels do not incur the diriment impediments established by the Church. Even when one of them is converted and baptized, the conversion and baptism do not effect the validity of the marriage. If the infidel husband is willing to live peacefully and not interfere with his converted wife in the exercise of her religion, their marriage cannot be dissolved. If, however, he be unwilling to do this, then the converted spouse may take advantage of the Pauline privilege mentioned in I Cor. VIII. After the interpellations have been made to him and he be still unwilling, or a papal dispensation from them has been previously obtained, the converted party may be declared free to enter other nuptials."

"I am convinced now more than ever," exclaimed the young woman, "that my case can be settled by the Church. That man John Betruger was never baptized; neither was I, but I intend to be. He ridiculed all religion and often said that church goers were a lot of hypocrites. What is there to prevent me from enjoying the privilege mentioned by St. Paul?"

"Oh, nothing," replied Fr. Michaels, "unless lack of evidence and the fact of your not being converted. How can you prove that you and your husband were never baptized?"

"Why, Mr. Paxton and I will make affidavits to that effect," she replied.

"Both of you being interested witnesses," said Fr. Michaels, "your testimony would be inadmissible in the Matrimonial Court of the Church. Affidavits of that kind are not worth the paper upon which they are written. Testimony doctored up at the instigation of the petitioners seeking the decree of nullity is thrown out of court. It hinders more than it helps. Church officials always insist upon documentary evidence when obtainable. They want a certified copy of a baptism or marriage from the original entry made in the baptismal or marriage register of the Church in which the ceremony took place. If the records have been destroyed, then the Court will be satisfied with two competent and trustworthy witnesses who have a knowledge of the facts and are willing to tell them truthfully under oath. The moderator usually cites these witnesses to appear personally before him on the day when the court convenes, in order that they may be thoroughly examined by him and cross-examined by the Defender of the Marriage Bond."

"But, Father," asked Miss Seymour, "supposing that the witnesses cannot come?"

"If they live quite a distance from the court, yet in the diocese where it convenes," said Fr. Michaels, "then the judge or auditor can delegate a priest living near them to take their sworn deposition and examine them. If they live outside the diocese where the case is being tried, then their addresses and interrogatories are sent to the Bishop of that locality. He usually authorizes his Vicar General or some other competent ecclesiastic to take down their sworn answers to the interrogatories forwarded."

"But must a regular trial precede the settlement of the case?" asked Miss Seymour. "I thought that the Bishop could decide it himself."

"Well," said Fr. Michaels, "in a case like yours, viz.: disparity of cult, or bigamy, consanguinity, affinity from marriage, spiritual affinity from baptism or confirmation, and clandestinity,— if the marriage is invalidated from such impediments — the Bishop can grant a decree of nullity without a trial provided he has previously heard the Defender of the Marriage Bond with whom he has carefully weighed the evidence."

"Well, what do you advise in my case?" nervously asked the young lady.

"Candidly, I am not over-enthusiastic," replied Fr. Michaels. "In order that I may present your case in due form before the Bishop having jurisdiction to decide it, kindly write a brief history of it when you go home. State when and where you were born and to what church you belong; when, where, to whom and by whom you were married, where and how long you lived together; when, where and why you were separated; give the names and religion of your and his parents. Tell whether you and he were ever baptized. Indicate names and P. O. addresses of two competent witnesses who have a direct knowledge of the facts concerning yourself and husband and are willing to give their testimony under oath. Of course the Church will not touch your case until you have become a member. Are you really in earnest about becoming a Catholic?"

"I was never more in earnest about anything in my life," she answered.

"As proof of your sincerity, then," said Fr. Michaels, "you must release Mr. Paxton from all obligation towards you and see as little as possible of him until after your admission into the Church. You must furthermore agree to abide by the Church's decision, no matter whether it be favorable or unfavorable."

"I am perfectly willing to promise all these things," she replied.

"Very good, then," said Fr. Michaels. "Kindly attend the 8 o'clock Mass to-morrow morning, after which I may introduce you to an estimable Catholic lady who will deem it a pleasure to help you through the catechism."

"How long do you think that it will take, Father, before I am admitted into the Church?" she anxiously demanded.

"That," said Fr. Michaels, "will largely depend on your application and progress."

CHAPTER V

RELIGIOUS INDIFFERENCE

"I hope that she is not trying to join the Church in order to marry Paxton," soliloquized Fr. Michaels, after the departure of his visitors. Marriage conversions were at a discount in his estimation. He regarded them as having a tendency toward hypocrisy, rather than genuine piety.

"Your dinner is getting cold, Father," said the housekeeper, appearing in the doorway of his study. "The Minchione boys telephoned to know if you cared to go sailing with them this afternoon. I replied that you were engaged with some persons in the parlor, and that I would ask you as soon as you came out."

"Call them up and say that I will be there at half-past two," replied Fr. Michaels. All through the meal his thoughts were centered upon the events of the morning. "I'll turn her over to Mrs. Grebma," he said to himself, "and after she has finished the catechism, I will know whether she is sincere." About two o'clock he donned a panama that had seen better days, and arming himself with a stout hawthorn to teach manners to impudent canines that might dispute his right of way, he strolled down the beach towards the Minchione cottage.

In almost every parish may be found individuals, who, when interviewed about church affiliations, reply that they are Catholics, yet they cross the church's threshold only on the occasion of a baptism, marriage or funeral. Gross immorality, the duty of restitution, or secret societies prevent the majority from the practice of religion. Apart from these may be found a coterie of nominal Catholics whose lives, in the estimation of the world, are beyond reproach. Temperate, honest, industrious and generous, they command the esteem of their fellowmen. In business they are the soul of integrity. Nor do they belong to any forbidden organization. They are devoted to their families, affable to their friends, and deferential to the clergy, an attack against whom they might vigorously resent. But as to the fulfillment of religious duties, they manifest the greatest apathy. Sunday for them is a day of sloth. It is spent in lounging about the house, perusing newspapers, playing golf or other amusement. Their religion is usually vested in the feminine portion of the household. Now to this category of indifferentists belonged the male members of the Minchione family. The parents originally from Sorrento, Italy, migrated shortly after their marriage, to Chicago, where their children — three sons and two daughters — were born and raised. The father's commercial career was meteoric. He began by peddling vegetables. Through patient toil and frugality, he managed after a few years to launch into the wholesale fruit business. The family returned each season to the island as regularly as the robins. Fr. Michaels visited them often in the hope of bringing them to a sense of duty.

"Buon giorno, Signori!"[1] he exclaimed, approaching the father and two sons, who were rigging a small sail boat that lay at anchor near the pier.

"Oh, favorite, Padre!"[2] replied the three, doffing their hats.

"No sailorman evah maka deesa knots," muttered the elder Minchione as he tugged impatiently at one of the gaskets. "Lika de ones Padre maka in de shoorsh."

"How is that?" inquired Fr. Michaels.

"Why, like the marriage knot which people make before you with their tongues and can't undo with their teeth," explained Rocco, the oldest son.

Fr. Michaels stepped lightly into the stern of the boat and sat alongside Mr. Minchione, who evidently intended to do the steering. "Well, Padre, watsa gooda news?" asked the latter as he headed the prow towards Bois Blanc.

[1] Good morning, gentlemen.
[2] Welcome, Father.

"Oh, nothing much," replied Fr. Michaels. "I didn't see you or the boys at Mass last Sunday."

"I guessa you're right," said Minchione, with just the faintest shadow of embarrassment. "But, Padre," he continued, "you can allus finda Mrs. Minchione anda girls in a shoorsh. Dey maka pray for whola famiglia."

"That won't do you much good on the day of final reckoning," said Fr. Michaels, "when each man shall be judged according to his works."

"Oh, I don't tink it maka mucha difference wit God Almighty whata man believa if he be honesta man," said Signor Minchione.

"Well," continued Fr. Michaels, "that is the shortest profession of faith I ever heard. It has the Apostles' Creed and Decalogue reduced to one commandment: 'Thou shalt not steal.' What would you think of a person asserting: It makes no difference whether I have eyes provided I see, whether I have ears so long as I hear, whether I have a tongue so long as I can talk, whether I have feet provided I walk? There is certainly something wrong with the brain of anyone uttering such language. Because without eyes, man cannot see, without ears he cannot hear, without a tongue he cannot talk, nor without feet is he able to walk. It is equally absurd to say: It makes no difference what a man believes, provided he be honest. What is your notion of an honest man?"

"Why," said Rocco, "the one who doesn't write Black Hand letters to his fellow countrymen, and who pays his debts."

"Such a person," replied Fr. Michaels, "might keep out of jail. But I would not regard him solely on that account as an honest man. One might go through life without stealing or killing, and yet be a blasphemer, drunkard and libertin. Did it ever occur to you that the religious indifferentist is both a thief and a murderer?"

"How do you figure that out?" asked Ralph.

"He is a thief," replied Fr. Michaels, "because he robs the

Creator of the worship due Him, and a murderer because through neglect of his religious duties he brings spiritual death and damnation upon his soul."

"Well, don't those live right, who do what they believe is right?" continued the young man.

"Not necessarily," replied Fr. Michaels. "With Luther, belief was everything and good works nothing. 'Sin fearlessly,' he said 'but believe more fearlessly.' The majority of our separated brethren have completely reversed the Lutheran motto. They claim good works to be everything and faith nothing. 'Believe what you like and do right,' says the indifferentist, which of course, is easier said than done. Our actions are very largely the outward expression of our belief. We cannot have a wrong belief very long without doing wrong. The Catholic Church has always taught that we must both believe right and do right. Common sense tells us that we cannot do right unless we believe right. Mormons believe in polygamy and keep several wives. Most Protestants believe in divorce or successive polygamy, which enables them to have several wives in rotation. Catholics believe 'what God hath joined together let no man put asunder.' Anarchists believe in the destruction of all organized government. It cannot be right living to follow the dictates of caprice. Those alone live right who live as God wills and commands. His Divine Will is revealed to us through 'faith which cometh through hearing.' The man without faith is ignorant of God's will. Hence he cannot live right. It was in order to teach us right living that the Son of God descended upon earth and established a church. 'Go ye into the whole world and preach the gospel to every creature. He that believeth and is baptized shall be saved. He that believeth not shall be condemned. He that heareth not the church, let him be to thee as the heathen and the publican.' If it makes no difference what a man believes, then the martyrs were foolish in refusing sacrifice to the idols; the Apostles should have remained in Palestine. They might just as well have ignored the divine command to evangelize the world, and the nations would still be enveloped in idolatry and superstition. It makes an awful difference what a man believes and whether he practices his belief. 'Not everyone that saith Lord, Lord, shall enter the kingdom of heaven, but he that doeth the will of my Father, he shall enter the kingdom of heaven. If thou wilt enter into life, keep the commandments.'"

"Do you think that all Catholics neglecting Mass and the sacraments shall be lost?" asked Ralph.

"The average man," said Fr. Michaels, "would regard it the height of folly to assume quarter the risk in business that you boys and your father are taking with the important affair of salvation. Our faith teaches that wilful neglect of Mass and the sacraments is a mortal sin and to die in that state means eternal perdition. Catholics ignoring their Easter duty, are deprived of Christian burial when they die. Their prospects on the other side are not very encouraging."

"And what about Protestants?" enquired Rocco.

"If they firmly believe in Christ, and are baptized," replied Fr. Michaels, "and honestly seek the one true religion, they can be saved. It won't be through their false sect, but through the Catholic Church, to the soul of which they belong, although apparently not members. Those failing through human respect or other worldly motives, to join the one true church in which they believe, cannot expect to be saved while in that state, for Christ has said: 'Whosoever shall deny me before men, I will also deny him before my Father who is in heaven.' Pagans, who never heard of the true church, nor had a chance to enter it, will not be condemned by reason of their unbelief, but on account of other sins committed. God will afford them an occasion to embrace the true faith rather than let them perish without their fault. The Catholic indifferentist cannot allege this pretext. God gives him ample opportunity to practice his religion. He has perhaps, the edifying example of his wife and children. Reverses in business, illness, or other misfortunes are providentially permitted in order to open his eyes to the importance of his salvation. Let him not be deceived by the vain hope of rectifying a sinful life by a deathbed repentance. At that supreme moment may be verified the words of our Savior: 'You shall seek me, you shall not find me, and you shall die in your sin.'"

CHAPTER VI

ONE TRUE RELIGION

"Heads down!" exclaimed Rocco, preparing to let the sail swing over to the other side. "A basso Zi Pre,"[1] he continued, in an effort at humor, "if that boom ever struck you, we could say: That was the blow that killed Father."

Fr. Michaels didn't need a second invitation, but promptly crouched down and crawled over to the larboard side as the boat veered around on the homeward tack.

"A short time ago," said Rocco, "I stopped to listen to one of those curbstone orators on North Clark Street. He claimed that every religion was good; that only bigoted, intolerant people want all men to adopt their mode of belief. All churches are just like the railroads to New York. You can take the Lake Shore, the Pennsylvania, Baltimore & Ohio, Wabash, Erie or in fact any road running east. So it is with the man wishing to reach heaven. He may select whatever denomination suits his particular fancy, because they all have heaven as their terminal. What do you think of that theory, Father?"

"Very plausible," replied Fr. Michaels, "at least to the ignorant failing to detect in it, what philosophers call begging the question, or asking us to take for granted what must be proven. It reminds me of an incident that happened in 1875, upon returning with my parents from a journey abroad. Scarcely had we landed than we were besieged by a horde of railroad agents. One of them made a most fervid appeal for the Baltimore & Ohio. 'Why for safety, comfort and natural scenery,' he declared, 'it is simply unsurpassed. It is the only

---

[1] "Down with Uncle Priest." "Uncle Priest" is a familiar title given the Clergy in Southern Italy.

route affording you an opportunity to behold one of the seven wonders of the world — the Great Niagara Falls!' His oratory thrilled my juvenile mind. 'Oh, let us go that way!' I exclaimed, in anticipation of the wonderful sight, having never seen the famous cataract, except in my geography. We went that way and didn't come within several hundred miles of the falls. It was one continual bump the bumps during the entire night, rendering sleep impossible. Although having left New York on Friday afternoon, we reached South Chicago about 7 o'clock Sunday morning where we remained until noon, waiting for a switch engine to come and pull away a derailed freight car that blocked the track. Now all churches do not lead to heaven any more than all roads lead to Niagara. Hence it is prudent to make sure beforehand that you are aboard the right train, that you are in the one true Church, else you may wake up in eternity quite a distance from the place you intended to reach. While there are several routes to New York, the only way of reaching Heaven is by the way of God's commandments and the precepts of His Church. 'If thou wilt enter into my life, keep the commandments. He that heareth not the Church, let him be to thee as the heathen and publican.' Our Lord never intended to establish or sanction various conflicting denominations. He desired one corporate body with all the members united under one visible chief. Since His Church is a visible body, it must have a visible head. 'I pray for them also who, through their word shall believe in me; that they all may be one as thou, Father in me and I in thee.' Our Savior prayed that His followers might be united in a common faith, just as He and the Father are united in one and the same divine nature. 'Be careful,' says St. Paul, 'to keep the unity of the spirit in the bond of peace; one body and one spirit, as you are called in one hope of your calling; one Lord, one faith, one baptism, one God, one Father of all.' The same Apostle exhorts us 'that henceforth we be no longer children tossed to and fro by every wind of doctrine. He places schism and heresy in the same class with murder and idolatry and declares that the authors of sects shall not possess the kingdom of God. Sects therefore, cannot have the same terminal as the one, true Church. Did you ever consider what religion really is?"

"No," replied Rocco.

"If you did," said Fr. Michaels, "you would see how stupid it is for anyone to assert that every religion is good. Religion is a virtue obliging man to render true homage to his Creator. Since there is but one Creator and the moral duty of rendering Him homage arises from one and the same absolute dependence upon Him which all men equally possess, it follows that religion must be essentially one. From the synagogue it passed to the Christian Church, just as the seed passing through the various phases of growth, finally develops into a majestic tree. If there was not one true religion, men could never invent false ones. Falsehood never exists alone. It presupposes truth. Spurious representations can only be made of the original. If there was not a genuine currency authorized by the government, counterfeits would be impossible. The children of Noah strove in their conceit, to reach heaven by erecting the tower of Babel. Their foolish enterprise culminated in the confusion and multiplication of languages. The so-called reformers of the XVI century endeavored to lead men to Heaven by the private interpretation of the Bible. Their efforts terminated in the confusion and multiplication of sects."

"Well, Father," said Rocco, "Protestants certainly know more about the Bible than we do. There is an apostate Italian in our neighborhood who can quote it by the yard."

"Oh," said Fr. Michaels, "if by *we* you simply mean individuals like yourself and brothers, who never hear the Word of God from one end of the year to the other, I readily concede. You certainly know less about the Bible than church-going Protestants. Practical Catholics know the Bible better and have a far deeper respect for it than their separated brethren. We regard it as the inspired word of God and firmly believe that He authorized the Church alone to interpret its true meaning. The Bible may be compared to the American Constitution. Individuals have no right to interpret it according to caprice, otherwise the republic would be of short duration. It would rapidly become like Protestantism, and we would soon be speaking, not of the United, but of the Divided States. All are bound to abide by the decisions of the Supreme Court. Our Lord established His Supreme Court and Supreme Judge whose duty is to give us the true interpretation of the Bible. He authorized the Bishops and priests of His Church to go forth and teach all nations. Like their Divine Master they speak as having authority, because they are furnished with credentials just as authentic as those given to the Apostles themselves. 'As the Father hath sent me, I also send you. He that heareth you, heareth me. He that despiseth you, despiseth me.' The indifferentist manifests his unwillingness to hear the Church. He displays the utmost contempt for her precepts by neglecting Holy Mass and the sacraments. According to our Divine Redeemer, he ought to be regarded in the same way as were the heathen and publican by the chosen people of Israel, viz: avoided and considered outside the pale of salvation."

"Eh, Padre," said the elder Minchione, as he held the gunwale of the boat close to the pier for him to land, "iss alla right. Whena we cooma to shoorsh, we cooma to Catolica Shoorsh."

"Yes," said Fr. Michael, "some day you will perhaps realize that while to eat, drink, sleep and gratify the senses may suit the animal kingdom, man was placed upon earth for a higher destiny."

CHAPTER VII

NUPTIAL MASS

St. Ann's Church presented a gala appearance. The altar always trim and tidy, seemed on this occasion more profusely decorated than usual with fresh cut flowers. Palms and ferns were tastily arranged about the sanctuary while the shelves of the altar presented a variegated mass of roses and nasturtiums, sweet-peas, lilacs and carnations. Four prie-Dieus occupied the space midway between the lowest altar step and the communion rail. There was to be a wedding that morning. Fr. Michaels had already vested and with two acolytes clothed in cassocks and snow white surplices, patiently awaited the arrival of the bridal couple.

"Father, they're coming!" excitedly whispered one of the boys, as the clatter of horses' hoofs and the creak of carriage wheels could be heard distinctly from the direction of the street.

"Well, light the candles," rejoined Fr. Michaels, "and be careful to not upset the flower vases."

Bride and groom had been to confession the day before and with their witnesses had carefully rehearsed the marriage ceremony. Fr. Michaels mounted the altar steps and turning around faced the congregation, as the nervous twain moved slowly up the aisle in rhythm with the majestic processional march that pealed forth from the organ. They made no pause until reaching the lowest altar step. Fr. Michaels reminded them of the sacredness of the union upon which they were about to enter — how our Lord raised marriage to the dignity of a sacrament, and annexed to its worthy reception special graces, thus enabling husband and wife to faithfully discharge their important duties. After joining them in wedlock they returned to their prie-Dieus, while Fr. Michaels began the Nuptial Mass. At the end of the Pater Noster they came forward and knelt on the lowest altar step. The priest turning around recited over them the first part of the Nuptial Blessing after which he continued the Mass. Having received Holy Communion they returned to their places where they remained kneeling in prayer and thanksgiving. Following the Ite missa est, Fr. Michaels turned around once more and pronounced over them the last part of the Nuptial Benediction: " May the God of Abraham, the God of Isaac, and the God of Jacob be with you, and may He fulfil His blessing upon you, that you may see your children's children unto the third and fourth generation, and may afterward have everlasting life, without end, by the help of our Lord Jesus Christ, Who, with the Father and the Holy Ghost, liveth and reigneth God, world without end. Amen." He briefly exhorted them to keep ever in mind the mutual love and fidelity they had pledged each other. " Walk constantly," he said, " in the way of God's commandments and the precepts of His Church. Let His Holy Will direct you in all your actions. It will enable you to bear each other's burdens. It will promote your happiness here and prepare you for a more lasting happiness hereafter." Then sprinkling them with holy water, and giving the customary blessing to the people, he finished the Mass. About ten minutes later as he proceeded down the aisle he noticed Miss Seymour in the lower end of the church and beckoned her to follow him. Mrs. Grebma was seated in an open carriage that stood at the front of the church.

" Good morning, Madame," said Fr. Michaels, as he approached her. " Allow me to introduce Miss Seymour of Chicago, who is spending the summer with friends at the East End." The ladies exchanged a formal greeting. " That was a very pretty wedding you had, Father," said Mrs. Grebma. " Don't you think so?" she continued, glancing toward Miss Seymour.

" Very impressive," replied the latter.

Nuptial Mass

"Miss Seymour is not a Catholic, but hopes to become one in the near future," said Fr. Michaels.

"Oh, what a pity, that we were not near each other during the ceremony," exclaimed Mrs. Grebma. "I would have loaned you my manual containing a translation of all the prayers recited. Fr. Michaels insists upon his parishioners being married at Mass. It adds so much solemnity to the reception of the sacrament and tends to make the married couple realize more fully the important step they are taking. Then there is the special blessing that is never imparted outside of Mass, is it, Father?"

"No, Ma'am. It can only be given during Mass," replied Fr. Michaels. "Afternoon and evening marriages are really an abuse that ought to be universally discouraged."

"I thought," said Miss Seymour, "that our Lord discouraged all external worship when He said: The hour cometh and now is when the true adorers shall adore the Father in spirit and in truth."

"When external worship expresses the sentiments of the heart," replied Fr. Michaels, "it is really adoration in spirit and in truth. How could our Lord discourage that which He Himself did and commended in others? When He fell prostrate to the ground before His Heavenly Father in the Garden of Olives, that was external worship, as was also the act of the publican striking his breast and exclaiming: Lord, be merciful to me a sinner. Don't you think that in both instances it was adoration in spirit and in truth? Striking the breast, making the sign of the cross, bowing and genuflecting are dictated by what we feel in our hearts. As to sacrifice, mankind with few exceptions, have always made it the chief act of religion. The prophet Malachy declared that the Jewish sacrifices were to be abrogated. 'I will not accept a gift from your hand. For my name is great among the gentiles. And in every place there is sacrifice and there is offered up to my name, a clean oblation from the rising to the setting of the sun.' In the Catholic Church alone, we find this prophecy accomplished in the daily sacrifice of the Mass. 'We Christians,' says St. Paul, 'have an altar whereof they cannot eat who serve the tabernacle.' If the Christian Church has an altar it must also have its own peculiar sacrifice, for the one implies the existence of the other. The priesthood of Christ was established to offer a distinct sacrifice. 'The Lord hath sworn and shall not repent; thou art a priest forever according to the order of Melchisedech.' Genesis tells us that Melchisedech, the king of Salem, brought forth bread and wine, for he was a priest of the most high God and he blessed Abram. Now at the last Supper our Lord took bread and blessed it and gave it to His disciples, saying, take ye and eat: 'This is my body which shall be delivered for you. He gave them also the chalice, saying: Drink ye all of this, for this chalice is my blood in the New Testament. This do ye, for as often as you eat this bread and drink the chalice, you shall show the death of the Lord until He come.' If our Lord did not exercise His priestly office on that occasion according to order of Melchisedech, He never did so, and hence could not be truthfully called 'a priest according to the order of Melchisedech.' In every place from the rising to the setting of the sun our Lord continues through the instrumentality of His priests to offer up the clean oblation of His adorable body and blood under the appearances of bread and wine in the holy sacrifice of the Mass."

"But doesn't the Mass derogate from the sacrifice of the cross?" asked Miss Seymour.

"How can it?" replied Fr. Michaels, "since it applies to us no merits of its own, but simply those of the cross of which it is a permanent memorial. Christ Himself established the sacrifice of the Mass and commanded His Apostles to celebrate it when He said: 'Do this for a commemoration of Me.'"

"Well," continued Miss Seymour, "why don't the priests say it in English so that the people may understand it?"

"The Apostles," said Fr. Michaels, "preached the gospel in Latin and Greek — the two languages then chiefly spoken by the civilized world. When they became dead languages and invariable, they were providentially suited to accurately express the doctrine of the Catholic Church that never varies, because it is divine. Living languages constantly changing are best suited for man-made churches whose members are continually 'tossed about to and fro by every wind of doctrine.' The devout Catholic has no difficulty in following intelligently the holy sacrifice of the Mass. He regards the celebrant as another Christ and the altar as another Calvary. The alb worn by the priest reminds him of the white robe with which Herod clothed our Savior in derision. The cincture, stole and maniple represent the chains and cords with which our Lord was bound. Every movement of the priest at the altar symbolizes some phase or other of our Lord's passion and death. Now Miss Seymour, here is a catechism. You may begin with the prayers and learn them by heart. Every practical Catholic recites them morning and evening. Take a chapter for each lesson and recite to Mrs. Grebma when convenient. When you have finished the catechism I will give you a post-graduate course."

"I am afraid," said Mrs. Grebma, "that I will make a very poor instructor."

"Banish all fear, Madame," said Fr. Michaels. "Anyone who graduated a pew full of grown-ups as you did, shouldn't have the word 'failure' in her vocabulary.

"Mrs. Grebma," he explained to Miss Seymour, "is deeply interested in an Italian Mission where Sunday School takes place after the children's Mass. The teachers have difficulty in keeping the grown people out of the church until after the dismissal of Sunday School. Some months ago three Italian men took possession of one of the pews. Madame addressed them in her most persuasive tone: 'Excuse me, Gentlemen, but you must vacate. You are usurping the places of the children.' The signori evidently did not understand, for they did not budge. 'Oh, well,' she added, 'if you wish to join the Sunday School you may remain. How many gods are there?' Next! Next! The question passed unanswered down the line and the trio passed quietly out the front door."

"Oh, I am hardly as exacting as Father would have you

imagine," said Mrs. Grebma. "Won't you kindly drive home with me, Miss Seymour?"

The latter accepted the invitation and as the carriage disappeared towards the village, Fr. Michaels entered his house.

CHAPTER VIII

CATHOLIC EDUCATION

"That was a formidable charge Bolce made in the Cosmopolitan against the universities," said Mr. Grebma to Fr. Michaels, as both sat one afternoon upon the veranda of the Wawashkamo Club House. "Some of the professors, he claims, have assailed the Rock of Ages. They reject the divinity of Christ and His miracles and repudiate the inspiration of the Bible. In fact, with their advocacy of free love, abolition of private ownership and other vagaries, they have turned their lecture halls into nurseries of socialism, anarchy and atheism."

"If his statements are false," said Fr. Michaels, "the universities may sue the magazine."

"There is little danger of a libel suit," commented Mr. Grebma. "Bolce attended the lecture courses for several years in those institutions before he began to attack them."

"What effect will his exposure produce upon the public?" asked Fr. Michaels.

"Oh, just a momentary sensation," replied Mr. Grebma. "The average Protestant will denounce Bolce as a muck raker, and wealthy Catholics will continue sending their boys to sectarian and state universities, unless some concerted action be taken by the bishops. Our people are fascinated by the social prestige which the diploma from such institutions affords their graduates. While the thought of having their boys under the guidance of atheistic professors may not be very encouraging, they smother the qualms of conscience with the assurance that their sons are immune and in no danger of being inoculated with pernicious theories."

"Yes," mused Fr. Michaels, "there is just the trouble. Fond parents imagine their blue-eyed Willie with cuffs on his trousers and a fried egg cap on his empty pate an angel without wings, who couldn't go wrong if he tried. Religion, however, tells a different story. It informs us that we all have been born in the state of original sin which darkened our understanding, weakened our will, and left in us a strong inclination to evil. We naturally tend towards the point of least resistance, and it is easier to yield to our passions than to oppose them. We chafe under restraint. Our natural propensities militate against law which restricts our liberty. Like the Hibernian desiring to join the party 'agin the governmint,' so we are naturally against whatever curtails our freedom. Youth doesn't need the encouragement of infidel professors to find the observance of the decalogue irksome. What effect will it have on the morals of our young men, if in the universities they be taught to despise what in childhood they regarded as most sacred? Will they keep the commandments better by being taught to regard them as the inherited experience of simian ancestors, or as the revealed law of God Who shall one day reward the good and punish the wicked? If our young people be instructed to consider conscience as a bugaboo, a survival of the ghost-scare period, it won't take them long to break through every mortal restraint. If, on the other hand, they be taught to regard it as the law of God, written on the heart of man and speaking to man with the voice of authority, then they will hearken to its dictates and try to lead virtuous lives."

"Well," said Mr. Inkstorm, a journalist, who had just finished a round of the links, and was settling with his caddie, "my boy attends the public school. I don't believe in forcing religion upon a child. This is a free country and when he grows up, he can choose for himself."

"Did you teach him to walk in infancy?" ventured Fr. Michaels.

"Oh, his mother taught him that stunt," replied Inkstorm.

"Too bad," rejoined Fr. Michaels, "that he was not allowed

to crawl on all fours until he grew up. You should have let him choose his own mode of locomotion."

"Why so sarcastic, Father?" asked Inkstorm, somewhat irritated.

"In order to impress the truth more forcibly upon your mind," replied Fr. Michaels. "By neglecting the religious education of your boy, you are exposing his soul to spiritual paralysis. That is a greater crime than the neglect of his physical development, since we must take more care of our soul than our body."

"Well," said Inkstorm, "in order to keep soul and body together, one must learn how to make a living. The great trouble with the parochial schools is that they teach too much religion and too little of the three R's."

"Your statement is not verified by facts," replied Fr. Michaels. "Our graduates compare most favorably with those of any secular institution. In addressing an association of public school teachers a prominent statesman recently asserted that there must be something radically wrong when, out of 440 applicants for admission to Annapolis, 330 failed to pass in reading, writing and arithmetic! The trouble with the public school system doesn't arise from the branches it teaches (excepting certain fads spasmodically introduced), but from the absence of moral training it fails to impart. While theoretically non-sectarian, it has practically become a promoter of socialism and agnosticism. Of socialism clamoring for the secularization of schools and the distribution of everything connected with them free of charge. Of agnosticism claiming to know nothing of God, and insisting upon teachers and pupils being placed in the same category of religious ignorance. It is not so long ago that a work on political economy was rejected as a text book from the High Schools of Chicago, because it began with the declaration that 'All natural wealth is due to the beneficence of God.' If you wish your boy to grow up ignorant of his duties to God, to his parents and to his fellowmen, you have selected the best school for that purpose. Catholics, however, will continue to send their children to Catholic schools, colleges, academies and universities. When they graduate they won't be freaks with big minds and little wills, with giant knowledge and pigmy morals, because the development of their character will not have been neglected. It is related in the story of Ben-Hur that, when obliged to row on the galleys of his captor, he requested to be changed occasionally from one side of the boat to the other. He wanted the muscles of both arms and shoulders to develop equally. He did not wish to reach maturity with the right biceps of a man and the left biceps of a baby. Likewise the Church desires a complete education of her children. She wants them to row on both sides of the vessel, on the will side as well as on the mind side. That is why she desires religion to enter into the daily curriculum of their studies. Why should we open every avenue of secular knowledge to our children and close the one leading to God? It is said that in the Mammoth Cave you can find fishes that have eyes and see not. No ray of light ever beamed upon their optic nerve. Hence those fishes spend their whole lives in obscurity and blindness. Shall our children grow up spiritually blind to the purpose for which they were created and to the means for its attainment, because the light of religious truth was not allowed to shine upon them during the impressionable age of innocence? Not if we can help it. We don't propose to make mammoth caves of our schools."

"But can't the children get enough religious instruction at home or in the Sunday School?" asked Mr. Inkstorm.

"No, they cannot," replied Fr. Michaels. "The majority of parents have neither the time nor qualifications to impart religious instruction. Nobody can give to others what he doesn't possess himself. We don't want our children to acquire the notion that religion is a Sunday luxury to be worn with their Sunday suit which is taken off again as soon as possible and carefully hung in the cedar closet until the next holiday. The juvenile mind must be impressed with the idea that religion is an everyday necessity, to be exhibited in our conduct at all times, that the ten commandments must be observed on week days just as well as the rules of grammar and arithmetic. How will they familiarize themselves with their religious duties if they only hear about them once a week? The Sunday School is at best a makeshift to supply the deficiency of religious education in the locality where no parochial school exists. Suppose your boy showed talent for law or medicine, painting or music. How much progress would he make in any of those branches, if allowed to study them but one hour a week, and at a time when he ought to be outdoors enjoying the fresh air with his playmates? It matters not whether he becomes a lawyer or a doctor, an artist or a musician, a merchant, mechanic or manual laborer, which is not dishonorable. Whatever trade or profession he adopts, he certainly has the sublime vocation to become a practical Christian, an honest, temperate, industrious and useful member of society. If he fails in the attainment of this vocation, upon whom largely rests the responsibility of his failure, if not upon the parents? 'He that hath not care of his own,' says St. Paul, 'hath denied the faith and is worse than an infidel.'"

CHAPTER IX

SECRET SOCIETIES

Fr. Michaels said Mass Sunday morning at six o'clock. This mass was familiarly known as "the Manitou Special," because it afforded those embarking on the steamship a chance to comply with the first precept of the Church. Fr. Michaels was to sail that morning for Chicago, en route for Pittsburg, where he expected to assist at the ordination of a young Benedictine and preach at his first mass. The purser, an exemplary Catholic with a predilection for priests, did not have much difficulty in persuading the pastor of St. Ann's to exchange his inside room for a parlor cabin. At precisely 8 o'clock the deafening sound of the whistle like the bourdon of a cathedral organ, reverberated through the Straits all the way up to les Cheneaux; the gang-plank was pulled ashore and the *Manitou* gradually receded from her dock, never turning her prow southward until she had cleared the buoy. A half hour later, while strolling about the upper deck, Fr. Michaels encountered Mr. Paxton comfortably seated in a corner and deeply absorbed in a novel. As the latter arose to greet him, the priest made two discoveries: Mr. Paxton wore a miniature square and compass in the lapel of his coat, and the book which he held in his hand was a salacious romance by Émile Zola. Fr. Michaels' gaze wandered with visible disgust from the Masonic emblem to the book, and as he was about to continue his promenade Paxton caught him by the arm and pleaded with him to remain. "There is really no advantage in my losing time with you," said the priest. "When you called at my house, you left me under the impression that you were a Catholic."

"Why, so I am, Father. What do you mean?" asked Paxton.

"By the symbol you have there on exhibition," said the priest, "you publicly profess membership in a society condemned by the Church."

"Oh," exclaimed Paxton, "I have not ceased to be a Catholic. I still believe in the Church."

"Yes," commented Fr. Michaels. "You still believe in ignoring her commands. You must be either a Catholic or a Mason. You cannot be both simultaneously because a Catholic Mason is a contradiction. You might as well claim to be a Catholic-Protestant or a Catholic-Jew."

"I fail to see what harm there can be for me to belong to the Masonic lodge," said Paxton. "It helps me socially and commercially. Masonry is philanthropic and benevolent just like societies thriving under the Church's sanction and protection."

"As yet," said Fr. Michaels, "you have probably not advanced beyond the Knife and Fork Degree. Hence to you the inner workings of the Craft are a sealed book. You derive all the harm that can be found in renouncing the rights and privileges of a free-born Christian. Masonry and its kindred organizations have been condemned not only on account of the slavery imposed upon the will of the members through the oath of blind obedience and secrecy, but more especially because while feigning to be 'the hand-maid of religion,' they are really striving to supplant the Church of Jesus Christ. Catholics are forbidden to join them for the same reason that they are forbidden to become Protestants of any denomination whatsoever. Secret societies with their chaplains and prelates, hymns and Bible, religious symbols and ceremonies have all the characteristics of a sect. In Europe Masonry is brazenly frank in its hostility to Christianity and to all the political and social institutions having Christian principles for their basis."

"But, Father," said Paxton, "you certainly know that

American Freemasonry is not atheistic or anti-Christian like the kind existing in continental Europe."

"Yes," replied Fr. Michaels, "I personally know prominent American Masons who would scorn to adopt the contemptible tactics of their Masonic brethren in Mexico, South America, Italy, France, Spain and Portugal. Yet according to its ritual the spirit of Masonry is supposed to be the same the world over. Why do they prefer to hold their meeting under the mantle of darkness rather than let their light so shine before men that we may all see their good works and glorify our Father who is in heaven? Their very title: Free-masons is a misnomer. They sacrificed their freedom by an ironclad oath binding them to keep mum the secrets of the lodge under pain of the most excruciating tortures. The vast majority of them are business and professional men, clerks, drummers and politicians who would scarcely recognize a mason's trowel if they saw one."

"You cannot deny that they do a lot of good," said Paxton.

"Yes," replied the priest, "especially to their own members. Whenever there is a civic function such as laying the corner stone of a court house, city hall, post office or public library, the fraternity is usually in the fore usurping the place of honor. From their prominence on such occasions one might imagine that these public edifices were financed by the Craft instead of by the tax payers. This aggressiveness should not be tolerated, for it is sectarian and un-American. Did you ever hear of the execution or life imprisonment of a thirty-third degree Mason? The machinery of justice usually stops short like grandpa's clock if Masonic influence manages to reach judge or jury. At one time only those labeled with a Masonic emblem could advance in political, professional or commercial life. Fortunately that period has passed. Nowadays employers do not require the Catholic applicant to renounce his faith before giving him a position of trust. They ascertain beforehand whether he is an honest, sober, industrious and practical Catholic. They know that if he robs his employer, the confessor will bind him to restitution before he can approach the sacraments."

"What about the Odd Fellows and Knights of Pythias?" asked Mr. Paxton.

"Both were specifically condemned by Pope Leo XIII," replied Fr. Michaels. "The term, Odd, in its obvious meaning, signifies queer, strange, eccentric. The candidate seeking the third and highest degree of truth in the Odd Fellowship, is asked: 'What he expects from the truth?' Answer: 'It will teach him his duty to God and his fellowman.' Those Catholics are certainly odd who join a lodge usurping the teaching authority of the Church. It was to the Apostles and their successors, and not to the Odd Fellows that our Savior gave the commission to instruct us in our duties to God and our fellowman. According to St. Paul, no man should take upon himself the functions of the ministry, but he that is called by God as Aaron was. The Knights of Pythias, ignoring the calendar of Christian saints and martyrs, had recourse to heathenism for a patron saint. The self-sacrificing love of Pythias was bestowed upon one man — his bosom friend, Damon. Pythian benevolence is restricted to one class, viz.: to brother knights prompt in the payment of their dues. Their benevolence is equivalent to that of an insurance company. The Pythian lodge, like that of the Odd Fellows, is a vestibule to freemasonry. The Catholic prostrating himself before a Pythian prelate, and swearing most solemnly 'to obey all orders that may be given by the council of ten,' forswears his allegiance to the Catholic Church and incurs excommunication."

"I was told," said Mr. Paxton, "that in 1896 the Pope revoked the condemnation of the Odd Fellows, Knights of Pythias and Sons of Temperance."

"You were misinformed," replied Fr. Michaels. "It was urged that a gross injustice had been committed against quite a number of Catholics who had joined these societies in good faith. Without rescinding the condemnation the Holy Father allowed an appeal to be made to the Apostolic Delegate in each particular case wherein these four conditions were verified:

"' 1. If the Catholic joined any of these societies before he knew of its condemnation by the Church.

"' 2. If there be no scandal arising, or if the scandal be removed by the timely declaration of the Catholic that his only motive in retaining membership is to prevent his losing the financial benefits to which he has a claim, and that he will abstain from all intercourse with the forbidden society.

"' 3. If he cannot drop his nominal membership without serious damage to himself or his family.

"' 4. There must be no danger of perversion for himself or family, and in case of death the forbidden society, as such, cannot take part in the funeral. The members will not be allowed to wear their insignia in the Church, nor will they be permitted to hold the burial service of their ritual in the house of the deceased or in the cemetery.'

" The concurrence of all four conditions does not mean that a bishop or priest can absolve such a person; it simply means that through his pastor or spiritual adviser he may refer his case to the Apostolic Delegate at Washington, who shall decide whether he may continue his nominal membership in the forbidden society and still approach the sacraments. Of course in danger of death a member may be absolved by any confessor, provided he promises to submit his case to the Apostolic Delegate in case of recovery, and to abide by the latter's decision. The true Catholic, having at heart his eternal salvation, knows that the Church for wise and prudent reasons has placed the ban of her disapproval upon these secret societies, and that she forbids her members to join them under pain of excommunication. The uncertain hope of temporal gain through the transgression of her precept will fail to fascinate him, for he will keep in mind the words of our Divine Redeemer: ' Seek ye first the kingdom of God and His justice and all these things shall be added unto you.' "

CHAPTER X

INDEX OF PROHIBITED BOOKS

The conversation was momentarily interrupted by the approach of the Captain.

"Good morning," said the latter, extending his hand. "Going with us all the way, Father?"

"Yes, Captain," replied Fr. Michaels. "I am bound for Pittsburgh and from there to Buffalo, where I hope to take the *Northwest* back to Mackinac."

"That ought to make a delightful trip, especially through the St. Clair Flats," said the Captain. Whereupon he mounted the companion way leading to the hurricane deck and disappeared in the pilot house.

"You seem to be well acquainted with the officers of the boat," remarked Paxton.

"Why not?" replied Fr. Michaels. "Most of them are Catholics and they never miss the six o'clock mass during the entire season. Where did you get that abominable book?" he continued, pointing to the volume on the chair.

"Oh," replied Paxton, "I just got it to pass away the time. It can't do me any harm. I'm no spring chicken."

"You are too tough to be accused of that," commented the priest, with a smile that rather softened the asperity of the remark.

Ignoring the thrust, Paxton mustered up courage to retort: "What right has the Church to dictate what we should or should not read?"

"Let me answer that," said Fr. Michaels, "by asking you what right the U. S. government has to exercise censorship over the press, or to forbid, under the severest penalties, the transmission of immoral literature through the mails? If the Church has a right to interfere in anything, it is in regard to the retention and perusal of literature which she deems likely to corrupt the faith and morals of her children. Nobody questions the right of the state to enforce the Pure Food and Drug Act, the abolition of the common drinking cup and other sanitary precautions for safeguarding the temporal life of the citizens. Why then should not the Church enforce similar measures for protecting the spiritual life of her members? The Church is a teaching authority and must, therefore, instruct. Our Lord made her a guide and hence she must lead. He appointed her the custodian of revealed truth and she must keep it intact. She is styled by St. Paul, 'the pillar and ground of truth.' She must resist then, all errors opposing truth. She is a religious tribunal and must settle all doubts regarding what we must believe and what we must do. No earthly power can change her from what she was originally intended to be by her Divine Founder. Catholics make profession of their belief in all this when they repeat in the Apostles' Creed: 'I believe in the Holy, Catholic Church.' But how could she exercise all these offices so essential to her nature and constitution if she had no right to declare: This book contains sound doctrine; that one does not?"

"I don't see," said Paxton, "how the Church will gain anything by treating us like children."

"Nor do I see," replied Fr. Michaels, "how we can gain heaven, unless we become humble as little children. The Church has always exercised a censorship over the books to be read by her members. In the Acts XIX, it is related how the Ephesian converts brought together at the instigation of St. Paul, their superstitious books to the value of 50,000 pieces of silver and cast them into the flames. In subsequent ages heretical writings were condemned according as they appeared. To guard the faithful against improper and dangerous reading, St. Pius V established the Sacred Congregation of the Index. While fostering literature, science and art, the Church has never allowed her children the indiscriminate reading of all kinds of books, pamphlets or newspapers. With the invention of the printing press came the present-day system of licensing books, viz.: the Nihil obstat of the Censor and the Imprimatur of the bishop in whose diocese a work on faith or morals is published. The Council of Trent formed a Catalogue of the most pernicious books extant at that period and the sovereign pontiffs have repeatedly warned the faithful against all literature prejudicial to their spiritual welfare. Pius X commands the bishops to do everything in their power to drive out of their dioceses whatever bad books may be there in circulation. We have then both the fact and the right confirming the Church's authority to interfere and act as judge in such matters."

"Yes," said Paxton with some bitterness, "the Catholic Church is about the only one curtailing its members in this respect."

"Methodists," rejoined Fr. Michaels, "claim the right for their conferences to proscribe whatever books their communicants ought not to read. Rarely can you find a strict Methodist or Presbyterian perusing a Catholic publication."

"As a matter of fact, Father," said Paxton, "wasn't the Index of prohibited books made for the weak and ignorant?"

"Ye shades of Samson and Solomon!" exclaimed the priest, "do you place yourself for a moment in the category of the strong and wise? Where the Church makes no distinction, we are not permitted to discriminate in the application of her ordinances. Goodbye to the laws, if such a flimsy reason sufficed to exempt us from their observance. Where is the man so lacking in self confidence as not to imagine himself capable of tending to his duty without the law's intervention? The average reader thinks of what he reads. A bad book cannot produce good thoughts any more than a bad tree can bring forth good fruit. The conscience of every Christian tells him that to familiarize himself with unclean literature, whatever may be the beauty of its form or the attractiveness of its style, is morally wrong. No one who really loves Jesus Christ can enjoy reading what tends to weaken Christian faith any more than affectionate children can take pleasure in hearing the vilification of their parents."

"The Church does not credit her members with much discernment," said Paxton.

"If our Lord wished us to rely upon private judgment in matters of faith or morals," replied the priest, "he would not have established a visible teaching authority in His church. In books against faith how easily a sophism is presented, a dogma derided, an historical fact distorted! How few Catholic readers have the mental acumen, the analytic faculty and erudition to refute subtle attacks upon their religion! There is your filthy romance whose author claims to depict life of the underworld as it actually is and truth cannot be immoral! Never was there a more infamous principle uttered. The minute details of a murder, divorce or any revolting crime, may be most truthful in their lurid description, yet most demoralizing to the reader. In the average up-to-date novel heroes and heroines are usually insipid, unnatural characters whose chief trait is some form of degeneracy. Intrigue, revenge, assassination, conjugal infidelity, divorce and suicide are vigorously applauded, while the opposite virtues are exposed to ridicule. How many young people whose health and virtue have been undermined through the continual reading of salacious fiction! The constant perusal of depraved literature renders the heart and soul morbid, the mind weak and sickly, the affections capricious and fickle, the whole man ill at ease, yearning for what he has not, and discontented with what he has. The misery of it all is that tons of this demoralizing rubbish encumber the shelves of our public libraries."

"They cannot do much damage while on the shelves," said Paxton.

"If men, women and children had not access to them," added Fr. Michaels, "but the public library is like the drug store containing all kinds of poison as well as healthful medicines. There is, however, this difference: while the conscientious pharmacist gives out poison only when filling a doctor's prescription and is bound by law to paste the label Poison on the bottle, any boy or girl may take from the Public Library a poisonous book the perusal of which may destroy both soul and body. If Catholics should firmly resolve to neither read nor buy a book, magazine or newspaper which they know to be bad, their action would greatly aid in removing immoral literature. It would erect the Christian conscience into a real censorship of the press. It would diminish the supply of bad publications by lessening the demand. The disreputable editor possesses a thick hide. He has, however, one vulnerable spot. It is his pocketbook. If, when he outrages public decency, Christians en masse should withdraw their advertisements from his vile sheet and cancel their subscriptions, the remedy would be most efficacious. Recently I saw a paper marked: HOME EDITION. The front page contained two views of a notorious danseuse scantily attired, with a detailed account of her iniquitous escapades. The average colored Sunday supplement is an abomination tending to debase instead of to elevate the rising generation. Parents should be just as solicitous about the literature of their children as they are about their company. An improper book or newspaper should not be left around loosely under their grasp any more than a keen edged razor or a loaded revolver. The library of a home is a sure index to its character."

CHAPTER XI

EXISTENCE OF GOD

As the *Manitou* neared Harbor Springs Fr. Michaels left his friend in order to view the scenery. The beautiful bay flanked on either side by wooded hills, the steam launches furrowing boisterously through the placid water and frail canoes skimming noiselessly over its surface, formed a most fascinating picture. The kaleidoscopic landscape aroused the interest of all on board, while the spectators on shore seemed to fix their attention on the *Manitou* as she proceeded majestically through the narrow draw to the inner basin. Here she managed to turn around, thanks to the frantic efforts of a wheezy asthmatic little tug that fumed and sputtered, careened and wobbled so alarmingly under its herculean task that it seemed more likely to capsize than tow its monstrous captive to the wharf. After a delay of ten minutes to take on freight and passengers, the *Manitou* resumed her voyage southward. Fr. Michaels devoted most of the afternoon and evening to the preparation of a sermon. About eight o'clock, while gazing in mute admiration at the full moon that shed a path of silvery light ahead of the ship, as if to guide her on her way, Mr. Paxton approached him and said: " Father, what a glorious night this is! Do you think there are any sincere atheists?"

" In the course of ages," replied Fr. Michaels, " a few discordant notes have been occasionally heard disturbing the general harmony of belief in God's existence. Atheistic clamors have usually emanated from individuals whose sole claim to notoriety is their infidelity. Their names do not appear upon the list of the world's heroes. Rarely if ever did any of them distinguish himself in the arena of science, art or literature. The handful of atheists from Epicurus down to the bibulous, blatant, blasphemous Bob, cut a sorry figure when compared to the giant intellects of every century who have professed their belief in God. There are two classes of atheists: the sensual and the proud. The former find the restraints of the decalogue and the menace of eternal punishment embarrassing to their bestial proclivities. Hence like the fool in Scripture, they say in their heart: ' There is no God.' The latter are so dominated by their own superiority that they cannot brook correction even when consciously wrong."

"Well," remarked Paxton, " should anyone ask me to prove that there is a God, I wouldn't know what to say."

"In that case," replied Fr. Michaels, " it would be best for you to say nothing or refer your questioner to a priest. If anyone told you that this boat made itself, you would conclude that he was either joking, or that there was something wrong with his brain. If this boat could not make itself, how could this wonderful universe bring itself into existence? Common sense tells us that there can be no work without a workman. From this axiom we infer that the works of nature needed a Master Workman, supreme and distinct from nature. In every part of the world we behold marvelous design, exquisite harmony and complexity of laws. Hence we conclude that back of all there must be a wise Designer, Harmonizer and Lawgiver. 'All things were made by Him and without Him was made nothing that was made.' Man could not create himself, for that would involve contradiction. If man created himself, then he existed. If he already existed, what need was there to create himself? If he did not exist, how did he manage to be? He existed then when he didn't exist; he was and he wasn't — an evident absurdity. If man could not create himself, what brought him into life? Let us ascend from generation to generation back to the first man Adam, with whom mankind began. If you say that the first man, Adam, also had a father and a grandfather and so on indefinitely, you fall into the absurdity of admitting an infinite series composed of finite parts. We see a limit to the present generation of men and we cannot avoid the conviction that there must be also a limit at the other end. We must eventually come to a fixed point, a definite beginning. This point, this beginning is the first man who could not create himself. He must, therefore, have been created by a Pre-existing Cause, an eternal, independent, necessary, infinite, personal Being whom we designate as God."

"Pardon me for intruding," said a mansard-browed passenger with a Bostonian accent, "but being a member of the legal profession, I find your conversation deeply interesting. May I ask a question?"

"Certainly," replied Fr. Michaels, "a half dozen if you like."

"Well," began the Bostonian, "I believe in God and that we are an expression of the Divine Mind, and —"

"Oh," interrupted Fr. Michaels, "you believe in Pantheism, that tries to make everything in this world a part of God. According to you, man with all his vices is an emanation of the Deity — a modification of His Divine substance. Your belief is a bundle of contradictions, for it confounds Creator and creature, infinite and finite in one substantial unity."

"Pardon," said the Bostonian, "but the confusion is in your belief which places boundaries to God's infinity by having Him create things outside of Himself."

"Your difficulty," rejoined Fr. Michaels, "proceeds from a false supposition, viz.: that beings of one order can limit beings of a different order. As well might you claim that loading the memory with facts can limit the stomach's capacity for food. The limited and limiting must have some point of contact, some community of nature, else the one cannot act upon the other. The finite nature of creatures cannot limit the infinite nature of the Creator."

"I have often heard preachers emphasizing the universal belief of mankind in God," said the Bostonian, "but that argument never impressed me."

"Why not?" asked the priest.

"Because," replied the Bostonian, "that universal belief does not exist. The Buddhists, the followers of Confucius and the Shintoists are estimated at 480 millions. Brahminism, the prevailing religion of Hindustan, has about 120 million votaries who adore the supreme Brahma, which is nature."

"Why, they must be co-religionists of yours," interjected Fr. Michaels.

"Pardon," continued the Bostonian, "add to the aforementioned, 230 million natives of Africa and Oceanica who practice fetichism, the most revolting and degrading form of idolatry. Altogether you have 830 million pagans. Where is this much vaunted general belief in God's existence?"

"Well, my dear friend," replied Fr. Michaels, "it is one thing to believe in the existence of an object, and another thing to have a correct notion of its nature. Your objection confounds the existence of God and His Divine nature. No intelligent Christian claims that mankind in general has a true knowledge of God's nature, but that men generally have believed in His existence. The pagan adoring the sun or the moon or other created object, acknowledges a Deity in them. Pantheist like yourself, he confuses Creator and creature in one substantial unity. To have any weight your objection should prove that these 830 million pagans do not admit in any shape or form the existence of a deity. Atheists have always been anomalies like the blind among men. The general belief in God cannot be ascribed to the prejudices of early education, because such a theory confounds cause with effect. Lessons imparted to children are not the cause, but the consequence resulting from the general belief of mankind. Nor can it be attributed to fear. According to infidels, when man saw the vivid flash of lightning, when he heard the peal of thunder, or felt the shock of an earthquake, his fervid imagination conjured up some invisible power he wished to propitiate. Marvelous indeed that people should retain their belief in God during the winter months the same as during April showers, and most of them never experienced the terrors of an earthquake. Finally this general belief cannot have been invented by legislators or priests. Not by the former, because all governments presuppose some sort of a religious credence;

nor by the latter, for how could they present themselves as ministers of God, if there did not prevail among the people a strong conviction of His existence? As well might one assert that ambassadors founded the governments they represent, or that children invented the idea of parents. There is but one way to account for this general belief. God enlightens with the light of reason every man that cometh into this world. We recognize the Creator from the contemplation of His works. He is clearly seen, being understood by the things that are made."

CHAPTER XII

THE MOST HOLY TRINITY

"How would you prove the Trinity from reason?" asked the Bostonian.

"To attempt such proof would be foolish," replied Fr. Michaels. "Of course, we need but open our eyes to be convinced of God's existence. The heavens publish His glory. The intelligent order throughout nature reveals the effect of His power, wisdom and providence. But the mystery of the Trinity transcends all human understanding."

"Well," began Paxton, "when I went to Sunday School—"

"Pardon," said the Bostonian, "I place little credence in what I cannot comprehend."

"An infidel once made a similar remark in conversation at table to the famous Lacordaire," rejoined Fr. Michaels. "Passing him a dish of omelets from which he had taken more than his share, he sneeringly observed: 'I never believe in what I cannot comprehend. That's reasonable, isn't it, M'sieur l'Abbe?'"

"'Kindly explain,' said Lacordaire, as he helped himself to the meager remnant on the plate, 'how heat which renders metal soft, has made these eggs so hard.'"

"'I can't,' retorted the infidel, somewhat confused.

"'Nor can I,' replied the Dominican. 'I notice that it doesn't lessen Monsieur's faith in omelets. Nature as well as religion abounds in mysteries which we believe without being able to understand. Even though the mystery of the Blessed Trinity surpasses our comprehension, we can easily show that it contains no absurdity.'"

"Isn't it absurd to claim that three are one, and one three?" asked the Bostonian.

"That depends entirely upon the point of view," replied Fr. Michaels. "It would be absurd to say that there are three Gods and only one God, or that in God there are three Persons and only one Person. But there is no absurdity in asserting that God is one in essence or nature and three in personality. Can't a thing be one in one respect and threefold in other respects?"

"Why, of course," said Paxton, clearing his throat, "why I remember when I —"

"Pardon me," interrupted the Bostonian, "but how can each of three Persons be God and yet have only one God?"

"If I could explain the HOW," said Fr. Michaels, "it would no longer be a mystery. Why should poor man, unable to fix his gaze for even a moment on the noonday sun without being almost blinded, vainly try to penetrate the infinitely dazzling nature of God? There is an endless variety of natural phenomena which we cannot comprehend, yet know to be facts. If we cannot solve the secrets of nature, why presume to fathom the mysteries of nature's God?"

"But no mention of the Trinity is made in the Bible," persisted the Bostonian.

"No one knoweth the Son but the Father," replied Fr. Michaels, quoting St. John, "neither doth anyone know the Father but the Son, and he to whom it shall please the Son to reveal. The word Trinity does not occur in the Bible; the doctrine, however, is not only foreshadowed in the Old Testament, but expressly declared in the New. Plurality of Divine Persons is implied in the words of Genesis: 'Let US make man to OUR image . . . Behold Adam has become as one of US.' And in Psalm ii, 'The Lord said to me: Thou art my Son, this day have I begotten thee . . . The Lord said to my Lord: Sit thou at my right hand.' Hypostatic or personal existence is frequently attributed by the prophets to the Word and Wisdom and to the Holy Spirit of God. The promised Messias called Emmanuel, the Great Counsellor, the Mighty God is really distinct from God the Father who sends Him into the world and implies plurality of

Divine Persons. But what could be more explicit than the command of Christ to the Apostles: 'Going, therefore, teach all nations, baptizing them in the name of the Father and of the Son and of the Holy Ghost?' In the name, i. e. in the authority, power and virtue which the three Divine Persons equally possess, mankind is to be regenerated in the sacramental waters of baptism. Here Father, Son and Holy Ghost are really distinguished from each other by the conjunction *and,* while the singular term — In the *name* — indicates that they have the same essence or nature. Those few words which we daily employ in making the sign of the cross the symbol of our redemption, refute the Arians, Socinians, Jews and Unitarians, in fact all modern as well as ancient unbelievers denying the unity of God in three distinct Persons."

"Well, I know," exclaimed Paxton in a final desperate effort to break into the conversation, "that when I used to attend Sunday School —"

"Like most boys you stayed away oftener than you went, I fancy," interjected the Bostonian.

"No Siree," hotly rejoined Paxton, "I was a regular attendant."

"Well, what happened when you went to Sunday School?" asked F. Michaels.

"Why the priest," replied Paxton, "told us how St. Patrick explained the shamrock to the Irish by means of the Trinity."

"That must have been rather interesting," remarked the Bostonian. "You, evidently, got the Sunday School lesson upside down."

"What do you mean?" asked Paxton with a scowl.

"You meant that the priest illustrated the Trinity by means of the shamrock, and not vice versa," said Fr. Michaels, coming to the rescue. "All comparisons howsoever striking are necessarily imperfect when applied to the Blessed Trinity."

"I don't understand," said the Bostonian, "how any analogy can be discovered between material things and these incomprehensible mysteries of religion."

"We have any number of analogies illustrating in a measure the Blessed Trinity," replied Fr. Michaels. "They enable us to understand at least how the mystery contains no contradiction. The sun gives light and heat. The sun, heat and light are really distinct, yet all three are of the same substance and began simultaneously. Man is one, yet threefold in his rational, animal and vegetative life. The human soul though essentially one is threefold in its powers of understanding, will and memory. A popular illustration with theologians is the following: Everyone begets a mental photograph or image of the object he wishes to understand. This image conceived by the human mind, is not self-subsisting, but accidental, transient and is called a mental word. Now God eternally knowing and comprehending His Divine Nature, begets an infinitely perfect image of His attributes. That perfect image is the Eternal Word, the only begotten Son of God. To Him St. John refers when he says: 'In the beginning was the Word and the Word was with God and the Word was God.' In God there can be nothing accidental or transient, since He is a Being infinitely perfect. Hence the Eternal Word is not accidental or transient like the mental word in creatures. He must be identified with the Divine Nature, yet distinct from the Father from Whom He proceeds. The Word has the same divine nature as the Father, yet being generated by the Father, He must be really distinct from Him who is Generator. The Word then has all that is required for personality, viz.: an intellectual, individual subsistence. In the language of St. John, 'He is the splendor of His Father's glory and the figure of His substance.' God has not only infinite knowledge, but also infinite love. Beholding the perfect expression of His attributes in the Eternal Word, He loves Him and in return is beloved by Him. This eternal act of mutual love is not accidental like the act of love in creatures. Divine love is identified with God's own nature, yet really distinct from both Father and Son from whom it mutually proceeds. It is therefore a distinct personal relation of the Blessed Trinity and called in Scripture the Holy Ghost or Spirit. To say then that in one God there are three Divine Persons is equivalent to asserting that God must be considered under a threefold respect: subjectively as God the Father knowing Himself; objectively as God the Son known by Himself and that is the Eternal Word or only begotten Son; finally, as a God loving Himself and beloved by Himself, viz.: the object of mutual love which is the Holy Ghost proceeding from both Father and Son as from one principle. These eternal, self-subsisting relations are what we Catholics regard as the three really distinct Persons in one God. Without belief in this dogma the mysteries of the Incarnation and Redemption are devoid of meaning.

CHAPTER XIII

DIVINITY OF CHRIST

"I've heard that word Incarnation repeatedly," said the Bostonian, "but never knew exactly what it meant."

"In the language of St. John," replied Fr. Michaels, "it means that the Word was made flesh."

"That leaves me just as much in the dark as before," said the Bostonian.

"I don't doubt it," rejoined Fr. Michaels. "The light shineth in darkness and the darkness did not comprehend it. What you need is a child's catechism. It would tell you that by Incarnation is meant that Jesus Christ the Son of God, the Second Person of the Blessed Trinity, was conceived and made man by the power of the Holy Ghost in the womb of the Blessed Virgin Mary."

"I have always had the greatest regard for the teachings of Christ," said the Bostonian, "although I have my doubts about His miraculous birth or Incarnation as you call it."

"And of course you do not believe that He was the Son of God," said Fr. Michaels.

"No," replied the Bostonian, "I think all those wonderful circumstances of His birth and the miracles ascribed to Him originated in the minds of His enthusiastic followers. In this age of enlightenment miracles are the greatest hindrance to the acceptance of Christianity."

"You differ radically from St. Paul, a much greater authority," replied Fr. Michaels. "He claims that the greatest obstacle to the gospel of Christ is pride of the understanding and pride of the heart. Pride of the understanding which prevents men from believing Gospel truths, pride of the heart which impedes them from observing Gospel precepts. Men embrace

Christianity to-day as in former times because it is authenticated by miracles furnishing it with irreproachable credentials and stamping it with the seal of divine approbation. The most of our knowledge is based upon testimony, that is, upon the confidence we place in the truthfulness of our fellowmen. We take historical facts for granted when confirmed by a multitude of disinterested witnesses who have nothing to gain, but everything to lose by deception. Such are the qualifications of the Apostles testifying to the occurrence of our Savior's miracles. The rejection of their testimony implies the repudiation of all historical certainty. The Pharisees did not regard miracles as a hindrance to Christianity. 'What do we?' they exclaimed, 'for this man worketh many miracles. If we let Him alone so, all men will believe in Him.'"

"For a miracle to occur," said the Bostonian, "the laws of nature would have to be set aside and that implies an impossibility."

"Yes, on the part of creatures," replied Fr. Michaels, "but not on the part of the Creator who made the laws. To deny the existence of miracles on the ground that they are impossible, is begging the question. It is like the argument advanced by the Siamese king when told by missionaries that in winter people of northern countries walked on ice or hardened water. He disdainfully rejected the assertion, 'because,' he said, 'everyone knows that it is impossible for water to get hard.' It is just as stupid for puny creatures to try to bind God's hands in His own creation and to limit His power."

"But," insisted the Bostonian, "in order to decide what event is miraculous, one would have to possess a universal knowledge of the efficacy of the natural laws."

"Not at all," replied Fr. Michaels. "We do not require universal knowledge to realize that no created power can, after the manner of Christ, restore sight to the blind, hearing to the deaf, appease the hunger of a multitude with a few loaves and fishes, or reanimate a corpse that has been decomposing for four days in the sepulchre. Our Savior wrought these miracles publicly and even in presence of His enemies."

"Well," said the Bostonian, "we can accept the sublime teaching of Christ without the miracles. Scientific thought has given us a civilization material, intellectual, moral such as the world has never before seen. Must we abandon this tremendous instrument for the advancement of mankind because of a few legends told by only a few observers in an age of boundless credulity?"

"My dear sir," rejoined Fr. Michaels, "you give scientific thought quite an amount of undeserved credit. To civilize means to reclaim from savage life and manners to a state of refinement and decency. Was it the scientists or the miracle believing apostles and their successors that civilized the Pagan world?"

"Why Great Scott," broke in Paxton, "were it not for the Catholic Church, you, like your ancestors, might be still living in a cave and wearing a bearskin and instead of sailing on this leviathan steamship, might be paddling around to-day in a dugout near the shore."

The Bostonian glared at him scornfully, but cowered immediately under the pugnacious gleam that lurked in Paxton's eye.

"Restrain yourselves, gentlemen," pleaded Fr. Michaels. "We cannot accept the teachings of Christ," he continued, "without accepting His miracles and His Divinity. To them He appealed in proof of it. His divine origin was the principal theme of His teaching. 'Whom do men say that I am?' He once asked the apostles. Simon Peter replied: 'Thou art Christ, the Son of the living God.' Our Lord sanctioned that answer. 'Blessed art thou Simon Peter, for it is not flesh and blood which have revealed to thee who I am, but My Father in heaven.' As a reward for his faith, he added: 'Thou art Peter and upon this rock I will build my church, and the gates of hell shall not prevail against it.' There is no middle ground to stand upon. We must either unite with the Pharisees in denouncing Him as a blasphemer or exclaim with Peter: 'Thou art Christ, the Son of the living God.' Have you ever read the Messianic prophesies?"

Divinity of Christ

"Never," replied the Bostonian.

"Well, when you reach Chicago," said Fr. Michaels, "go to a Catholic bookstore and get 'Christ in Type and Prophecy,' by Fr. Maas. It will teach you how the history of the chosen people of Israel is little else than a series of prophetic events, typifying various incidents in the life of the Messias. You will learn how God revealed, through His prophets centuries beforehand, the minutest details of our Savior's birth, His public career, His ignominious passion and death, and His glorious resurrection."

"But what assurance have you," asked the Bostonian, "that those prophecies are genuine?"

"If they were spurious," replied Fr. Michaels, "do you think that they would be retained by the Jews? Just to preclude objections of this kind it happened providentially that Ptolemy Philadelphus, king of Egypt about 250 years before Christ, ordered seventy of the most learned men of Israel to compile a Greek version of the Old Testament. Since before that period the prophets had long ceased to prophecy, it follows that there is not a single Messianic prediction that is not contained in that famous Septuagint translation of the Bible."

"How do you account then for the fact," said the Bostonian, "that most of the Jews repudiated Christ?"

"Their spiritual blindness and obduracy were the fulfillment of a prophecy," replied Fr. Michaels. "Their dispersion and social ostracism, the destruction of their temple and city were foretold as a divine chastisement for their crime of deicide. 'His blood,' they said, 'be upon us and upon our children.'"

"Who knows," said the Bostonian, "but that Christ may have studied the prophecies attentively and then adapted His life in accordance with them?"

"Marvelous!" exclaimed Fr. Michaels. "Don't you realize that such a prodigious undertaking would require the power of a God? What mortal could select his own mother? the precise time and place of his birth? the name to be given him eight days after his birth? What created being could find a Judas who would betray him for exactly 30 pieces of silver? Who among men could so pre-arrange the gibes and insults of his executioners, the laceration of his hands and feet, the division of his garments, the time of his death and resurrection? Who but God incarnate could emerge from the portals of death, be acknowledged and adored as the Divine Redeemer of mankind, not for a short interval nor merely in one locality, but for 19 centuries and throughout the civilized world? In Christ alone these wonderful events have been accurately accomplished according to their prediction. At the time of His crucifixion the eclipse of the sun, the earthquake, the rocks rent asunder, the dead arising and appearing to many, in a word, the convulsion of the elements seemed to re-echo the conviction of the Roman centurion exclaiming: ' Indeed this was the Son of God.' "

CHAPTER XIV

THE REDEMPTION

"If Christ were really God," said the Bostonian, "why didn't He prevent all the humiliation and suffering heaped upon Him?"

"His enemies asked the same question at the time of His crucifixion," replied Fr. Michaels. "'If thou be the Son of God,' they exclaimed, 'come down from the cross and we will believe in thee. He saved others; himself he cannot save.' In fulfillment of the prophecies, He had to suffer before entering into His glory. The 21st and 68th psalms vividly describe His passion and crucifixion. 'They dug my hands and feet. They numbered all my bones. . . . They parted my garments amongst them; and upon my vesture they cast lots. . . . All they that saw me, have laughed me to scorn. They have spoken with the lips and wagged the head. . . . They gave me gall for my food and in my thirst they gave me vinegar to drink.' I presume you have heard of the Redemption of mankind?"

"Oh, yes," replied the Bostonian, "it is what Protestants call the Atonement."

"Precisely," rejoined Fr. Michaels, "although the term — redemption, strictly speaking, implies really more than atonement or satisfaction for sin. By redemption we Catholics understand the restoration of fallen man from the slavery of sin to the freedom of God's adopted children through the atonement and merits of Christ."

"Don't the Modernists claim that the doctrine of Christ's atonement originated with Paul of Tarsus and is not found in the gospels?" asked the Bostonian.

"Yes," replied Fr. Michaels, "and their heresy was condemned by Pius X in 1907. Although the best explanation of the doctrine is given by St. Paul, he did not originate it, because it is mentioned not only in the gospels, but also in the Old Testament."

"I can't see any justice in punishing us for a sin committed by another age before we were born," said the Bostonian.

"Neither could I," replied the priest, "if the punishment consisted in depriving us of some faculty due our nature, as Luther maintained. According to him, original sin completely destroyed our free will. God certainly had the right to bestow His gifts on such conditions as He pleased and to make their conservation depend upon the fidelity of Adam, the head of the human race, just as an hereditary title might be conferred upon you and your children for generations to come, provided you observed a certain law. Through Adam's disobedience we share in his sin and punishment, as we should have shared in his happiness had he remained faithful. The punishment consists in the privation of supernatural gifts to which our nature has strictly no right, viz.: complete mastery over our passions, exemption from death, sanctifying grace and the beatific vision. Where is the injustice? Now God did not abandon man after his fall, but promised him a Redeemer in the person of His only begotten Son. He was to amply satisfy Divine Justice for the offense given and regain for us the right to heaven which we forfeited."

"Well, to redeem, as I understand it," said the Bostonian, "means to ransom, to buy back. If through sin we became children of wrath, slaves of the devil, then the ransom should be paid to him holding dominion over us, viz.: to the devil."

"Every comparison limps when carried to extremes or insisted upon too literally," rejoined the priest. "As a matter of fact the devil acquired no right over fallen man and was entitled to naught but punishment for having deceived him. The idea of paying Satan the purchase price of our redemption is ridiculous as well as blasphemous. God alone was offended by sin. Therefore to Him alone should reparation be made."

"But," insisted the Bostonian, "couldn't God have forgiven the offense without exacting any reparation?"

"Certainly," replied the priest, "but just now it is not a question of what God could have done, but what He actually did. He required complete atonement through the sacrifice of His only begotten Son."

"Pardon me," said the Bostonian, "but His Son was God, was He not? Hence He made atonement to Himself. Doesn't that sound absurd?"

"Yes," replied the priest, "it must sound absurd, especially to anyone inclined to quibble, but not to a candid mind anxiously seeking the truth. The county collector can pay and issue a receipt to himself for the taxes on his property. Do you notice any absurdity in the transaction because both payer and receiver happen to be one and the same person under different aspects? In our Lord's sacrifice all conditions necessary for an adequate satisfaction were fulfilled. He assumed, not the guilt, but the punishment of our iniquities. He made atonement to the Father and the Holy Ghost and to Himself considered in His divinity as morally distinct from the same divine person as incarnate."

"But why did He suffer such a frightful death?" asked the Bostonian.

"To teach us the enormity of sin and show His infinite love for mankind," replied the priest. "No creature could repair the injury committed against the Creator. Did you ever hear the juridical axiom: '*Honor in honorante, injuria in injuriato?*'"

"That's too deep for me," replied the Bostonian.

"Excuse me," replied the priest, "I thought, that being a lawyer your legal lore extended beyond the examination of deeds and abstracts. The axiom means that honor is measured by the dignity of the one conferring it, while injury is gauged by the dignity of the person injured. In other words, the more exalted the individual offended, the greater the offense. An insult offered to the President would be certainly greater than if directed against a street urchin. On the other hand the more abject the condition of the person atoning, the less is the value of his atonement. Now the distance between the offended Creator and the offending creature renders the malice of the latter's offense in a measure infinite. Adequate satisfaction therefore could only be effected by a person of infinite dignity. Any atonement attempted by sinful man would be worthless, because it derives its intrinsic value from the dignity of the individual atoning. Atonement, moreover, implies some act of self-abasement or humiliation. Now Christ, as God according to His divine nature, could not undergo humiliation, for that would imply an imperfection in the God-head. Hence He united to His divine person a human nature in which He could suffer and atone as man. Although impeccable He should hold a sort of middle ground between innocence and guilt. He should be really just in order that His atonement might have value, and apparently a sinner in order to incur a sinner's punishment. Hence according to St. Paul, 'God sent His Son in the likeness of sinful flesh.' Christ had the appearance of sin without ever having incurred its guilt. It was of Him Isaiah said: 'The Lord hath laid on Him the iniquity of us all.' (liii-6.) Of Him the Apostle declared: 'He hath delivered Himself for us an oblation and a sacrifice unto God.'" (Eph. v-2.)

"If He redeemed all men," said the Bostonian, "then no one can be lost."

"Nobody coöperating with the graces gained through the Redemption can be lost," replied Fr. Michaels. "The most efficacious remedy would not help an invalid unless he made use of it. Likewise the fruits of Christ's redemption will not benefit us, unless applied to our souls through prayer and the sacraments."

CHAPTER XV

THE BLESSED VIRGIN

"Catholics believe in the divinity of the Virgin Mary, don't they?" asked the Bostonian.

"No," replied Fr. Michaels, "they regard as an article of faith that she is the Mother of God."

"Well, that amounts practically to the same thing," retorted the Bostonian. "How could she be the mother of God unless she were divine?"

"She need not be divine in order to become God's Mother, according to His human nature," rejoined Fr. Michaels. "The same divine Person Jesus Christ, the Son of God, is also her Son. Therefore, she is the Mother of God. The better we understand her part in the mystery of the Incarnation, the more enlightened we become in regard to our Savior Himself. In fact the dogma of the Incarnation is epitomized in the glorious name, 'Deipara,' viz.: Mother of God. Nestorious refused the Blessed Virgin that title, because he placed in Christ a dual personality, while our faith teaches that He is but one Person with two natures, the nature of God and the nature of man."

"Well, I don't see," said the Bostonian, "how she can be rightfully called the Mother of God, if she did not give Him His divine nature."

"How can any woman be rightfully called the mother of her son," asked Fr. Michaels, "if she does not give him his spiritual, immortal soul? The terms mother and son are predicated of persons, and not of the elements composing them. We never say: 'the mother of our body,' although we are composed of a body derived from our mother's womb and of an immortal soul directly created by the Almighty. Now the

Blessed Virgin conceived of the Holy Ghost and communicated to the Eternal Word, i. e., the Son of God, a true human nature of the same substance as her own. His human nature is not divested of personality. God incarnate did not blossom out into a human person. The person of Christ is not human, but divine. The Blessed Virgin is not the mother of a human son received into union with God, for that was the heresy of the Nestorians and Adoptionists. They claimed that the human nature of Christ had a human personality. Of course human nature cannot exist without being individualized, without a personality. The Second Person of the Trinity supplied our Lord's human nature with personality. That which was conceived and born of the Blessed Virgin Mary was the Second Divine Person Who assumed or united to Himself a human nature. Therefore she is really and truly the Mother of God, just as much as any woman is the mother of her son. 'The Holy, which shall be born of thee shall be called the Son of God.' (Luke i, 35.)

"I have noticed," said the Bostonian, "that you Catholics invariably speak of her as the *Blessed* Virgin."

"Yes," replied the priest, "we take very great pleasure in honoring her whom God has signally honored by selecting her in preference to all other women, to become the Mother of His only begotten Son. Did you ever hear of the Magnificat?"

"No, what is it?" asked the Bostonian.

"It is the canticle uttered by the Blessed Virgin when visited by her cousin, St. Elizabeth. You will find it in the first chapter of St. Luke's Gospel. In the Latin Vulgate it begins with the word, Magnificat. 'My soul doth magnify the Lord and my spirit hath rejoiced in God my Savior. Because He hath regarded the humility of His handmaid. For behold from henceforth all generations shall call me blessed.' For the accomplishment of this prophecy we need not look among the generations of Protestants. For in speaking of her they usually withhold the title of 'Blessed,' preferring to call her the Virgin or simply Mary. From the zeal manifested by some sectarians in parading her alleged imperfections and ignoring her exalted virtues, one might imagine that our Lord took keen delight in listening to the vilification of His Mother! Evidently such traducers have no desire to be reckoned among the generations predicted to call her blessed. Perhaps they prefer to be counted among the generations of the fallen angel to whom God said in the garden of Eden: 'I will put enmities between thee and the woman . . . she shall crush thy head.' "

"Well, now," said the Bostonian, "let us have a little light on the subject. I want your candid opinion of a passage that I have marked in my Bible." They proceeded to the cabin, where the Bostonian produced a New Testament and began to read from St. Mark's: 'Is not this the carpenter, the son of Mary, the brother of James, and Joseph, and Jude, and Simon? Are not also his sisters here with us? And they were scandalized in regard to him.' I guess," said the Bostonian, triumphantly, "that Mary or the Blessed Virgin, as you call her, was the mother of quite a large family."

"You had better guess again," replied the priest, "for you certainly missed it the first time. Those so-called brothers and sisters of Jesus were not the offspring of the Blessed Virgin, but the children of a certain Cleophas by an altogether different Mary. The James mentioned in your text is called James of Alpheus (Matth. x, 3; Mark iii, 18), and the mother is called 'Mary the mother of James the less and Joseph. (Matth. xxvii, 56; Mark xv, 40). As Mary of Cleophas was the kinswoman of the Blessed Virgin, James and Joseph are called the brothers of Jesus, because the Jews had the custom of giving that title to cousins or near relatives. Lot was the nephew of Abraham, yet Abraham calls him brother. (Gen. xiii, 8.) Laban was both the uncle and father-in-law of Jacob, and yet Jacob calls him brother. (Gen. xxix, 15.) You might as well try to trace fraternal relationship between me and my congregation, for I usually address them as 'Beloved Brethren.' Mary was a Virgin before our Savior's birth, because the Gospel says so. 'Behold a virgin shall conceive and shall bring forth a son, and his name shall be called Immanuel, which being interpreted is God with us.' She is called a virgin in the Apostles' and Nicene Creeds which were compiled long after her death. Hence the term, virgin, cannot be restricted to the time of our Lord's birth, but must include her entire life."

"Was not Christ called 'her first born son'?" asked the Bostonian.

"Yes," replied Fr. Michaels, "in conformity with the ancient custom of thus designating the first born son of every Jewish mother, whether other children followed or not. Machir is called the first born of Manasses, although he was his only son. (Josue, xvii-i.)"

"But," insisted the Bostonian, "the gospel declares that 'Joseph took unto him his wife and he knew her not *till* she brought forth her first born son.' Hence we must conclude that after the birth of her first born, she had other offspring."

"We must not conclude anything of the sort," replied Fr. Michaels, "if we have any regard for logic."

"How do you figure that out?" demanded the Bostonian.

"We cannot draw an affirmative conclusion from a negative premise," rejoined the priest. "I am afraid that you are not very familiar with syllogistic architecture. The conjunction, till, does not imply that the chaste union between the Blessed Virgin and St. Joseph ceased to exist after our Savior's birth. In the text: 'The Lord said unto my Lord: sit thou at my right hand *until* I make thy enemies thy footstool,' would you conclude that after the subjugation of his enemies, our Lord no longer sat at the right hand of God? In other words, our Savior, according to His sacred Humanity, no longer occupied the highest place in heaven next to God?"

"All true Christians," said the Bostonian, "regard Christ as the one mediator who gave himself a redemption for all."

"Yes, He is the only mediator in the sense of Redeemer," replied Fr. Michaels. "But that does not prevent our asking the Blessed Virgin to pray for us. It was at her request that our Lord performed his very first miracle at the marriage feast of Cana. Her intercession is based upon the merits of Christ Who gives it value."

"But why bother with her intercession?" insisted the Bostonian. "God Himself can hear us. Why not pray directly to Him?"

"Your difficulty proves too much," replied Fr. Michaels. "Therefore it proves nothing. Why should we pray even directly to God, since He knows our wants from all eternity? Because a devotion is not absolutely necessary, we cannot conclude that it is useless. If it be wrong to seek the Blessed Virgin's intercession, then St. Paul made a great mistake in asking the Romans and Ephesians to pray for him; then we all are wrong in praying for each other, and the article: 'I believe in the communion of saints,' should be stricken from the Apostles' Creed. Our devotion to the Blessed Virgin does not derogate from the mediatorship of Christ, for the petitions addressed to her terminate with the formula: 'Through Christ, our Lord.' Nor does it infringe upon the adoration due exclusively to God. In praying to her we join with the archangel Gabriel exclaiming: 'Hail full of grace, the Lord is with thee.' (Luke, i.) We imitate St. Elizabeth, the holy spouse of Zachary and mother of St. John the Baptist, and with her we say: 'Blessed art thou among women and blessed is the fruit of thy womb.' We unite our voices with the One, Holy, Catholic and Apostolic Church in the petition: 'Holy Mary, Mother of God, pray for us sinners, now, and at the hour of our death. Amen.'"

CHAPTER XVI

FALLACY OF CHRISTIAN SCIENCE

The conversation proved too much for Paxton, who fell asleep in his chair.

"Are you not a Christian Scientist?" asked Fr. Michaels of the Bostonian.

"Yes," replied the latter. "How did you surmise it?"

"From your pantheistic notion of God," rejoined the priest. "You asserted that we all are an expression of the Divine Mind. That is the typical Christian Science jargon."

"But," protested the Bostonian, "you did not let me explain. Christian Science has nothing in common with pantheism, which places God in matter. Everything good is an expression of the Divine Mind."

"And what about everything bad?" asked the priest.

"There is nothing really bad," replied the adherent of Eddyism. "Sin and sickness are simply delusions of mortal mind. They do not exist any more than darkness or the color black. Darkness is the absence of light, while black is the negation of all color."

"Your explanation doesn't explain," replied Fr. Michaels. "Sickness and sin do not, of course, exist by themselves as distinct entities. Yet both are real modes of being. Do you regard the condition of a drunkard, leper, or murderer simply negative as to the absence of sobriety, health or virtue?"

"Christian Science regards these conditions as false concepts of mortal mind," rejoined the Bostonian.

"Then," exclaimed the priest, "it is foolish for the civil authorities to order quarantine and other sanitary precautions against leprosy, cholera, yellow fever and the like which are purely imaginary. We might also abolish capital punishment and tear down the prisons. Why try to repress or punish crime which really doesn't exist outside of mortal mind? What do you mean by mortal mind?"

"Mortal mind," rejoined the Bostonian, rolling his optics piously towards the sky, "is the human mind rebelling against the Divine Mind. It is the 'carnal mind' and the fruitful source of all sin and sickness. We believe in the eternal reality of one Divine Mind and the absolute nothingness of everything else. Oh, Brother!" he continued in gushing tones, "could anything be more sublime? You should read Mrs. Eddy's 'Science and Health,' and 'Key to the Scriptures' in order to appreciate the beauties of Christian Science."

"Excuse me," said Fr. Michaels, "I am not a brother, but a priest. Let me recommend to your serious perusal the arraignment of Christian Science before the Bar of Reason by Fr. Lambert. I once made an heroic effort to read that book supposedly written by Mrs. Eddy. All that I could appreciate were its glaring inconsistencies. Anyone comparing the stilted, ungrammatical prefaces accredited to her with the polished diction of the main part, will be convinced that she never wrote the book. Mark Twain claims that she had the commercial instinct abnormally developed when she demanded $300.00, payable in advance, for seven lessons in the art of healing. According to him, the three dollar edition of 'Science and Health' costs about 15 cents, while the six dollar de luxe edition averages 80 cents per copy. Seven hundred per cent. profit on these publications is quite a snug investment."

"The laborer is worthy of his hire," said the Bostonian. "You should respect Christian Science for at least the good it has accomplished."

"The laborer," rejoined Fr. Michaels, "has no license to practice extortion. As to the alleged good accomplished by Christian Science, you would have quite a task proving it, since it only cures evils that do not exist. Besides, we are never allowed to do evil that good may result therefrom. Like Carrie Nation, Mrs. Eddy sallied forth, axe in hand, and did not stop until she demolished every vestige of Christian faith — the Unity and Trinity of God, the Divinity of Christ with Whom she had the blasphemous effrontery to place herself on an equality; fasting, prayer and the Decalogue which she reduced to a sort of trialogue forbidding the use of tobacco, alcohol, and other drugs. 'Who,' she says, 'can conceive either of three persons as one person, or of three infinities as one infinity?' Such an absurd conception is as far from the Catholic doctrine of the Trinity as heaven is from earth. 'There is a dual personality in Christ,' she exclaims, 'the unseen and the seen, the spiritual and the material, the Christ and Jesus.' Too bad that she didn't flourish in the fifth century. Nestorius would have adopted her as his own, even though she basted on a few flounces to his heresy. 'Fasting,' she declares, 'is a senseless belief and Christ never fasted,' although the Gospel assures us that He fasted forty days in the desert. 'Prayer,' she claims, 'is unnecessary, as the All has already decreed what is good for us.' Her paraphrase of the Lord's Prayer beginning with: 'Our Father-Mother God, all harmonious,' is truly idiotic as well as Eddyistic. I cannot have respect for a cult that is a tissue of contradictions. It is neither Christian nor science. Not Christian, for it denies the fundamental truths of Christianity. Nor science, because science is a systematized body of knowledge whose various parts harmonize like the parts of a machine and admit of demonstration."

"Christian Science," retorted the Bostonian, "demonstrates its worth by the countless cures it has effected. 'By their fruits ye shall know them.'"

"If all sickness is a delusion of mortal mind," asked Fr. Michaels, "how can you cure what does not exist? The chief fruits by which the followers of Christ may be known, are the fruits of charity. What charitable works have thus far distinguished the Christian Scientists? Could you mention a single orphanage, asylum or refuge for the poor, the aged or the outcast, founded and supported by your marvelous cult? Do you know of any St. Vincent de Pauls or Father Damiens among your followers? How does the charity of your much married foundress 'Mother Mary,' 'Pastor Emeritus' and self-styled 'God's Little One' compare with that of Mother Catherine Drexel who, instead of squandering her fortune in pomp and luxury, is devoting her life and earthly goods to the uplifting of the Indians and Negroes? What a contrast Mrs. Baker-Eddy forms with Nathaniel Hawthorne's daughter, Sister Rose, who, although raised in culture and refinement, has consecrated her energy and talents to alleviating the sufferings of those afflicted with incurable cancer!"

"Works of charity," said the Bostonian, "arise mostly from sickness and sin. Christian Science abolishes the need for charity by removing its cause."

"Oh, I see," said Fr. Michaels. "You remove the need by denying its existence! A very simple process. If a hungry man asks for food, you don't reach him a stone or a serpent, but something less substantial. His limp and empty stomach you inflate with a little Christian Science hot air. You persuade him that he isn't hungry, but laboring under a delusion of mortal mind and send him on his way rejoicing."

"Doesn't the Catholic Church believe in healing the sick by faith?" asked the Bostonian.

"Certainly," replied the priest, "for we read it in St. Mark, VI, 13, and XVI, 18, that 'they anointed with oil many that were sick and healed them.' . . . 'They shall lay their hands upon the sick and they shall recover.' The Roman Ritual has a special prayer for nearly every ache and pain afflicting the human race. Relying on the promises of Christ, we firmly believe in the efficacy of prayer. 'Ask and you shall receive.' 'If you ask the Father anything in my name, He will give it you.' If we do not always obtain what we ask it is either because our prayers lack faith, humility and perseverance, or because God foresees that what we seek would be detrimental to our spiritual welfare. Following the injunction of St. James, we administer the sacrament of Extreme Unction, which through the anointing and prayer of the priest gives health and strength to the soul and even sometimes to the body when we are in danger of death from sickness. No Catholic priest, however, counsels the patient, as you do, to avoid the natural means at his disposal. Natural remedies are not to be disregarded when supernatural aid is invoked. God helps those who help themselves and He usually works His wonders through the established laws of nature. He doesn't want us to despise hygiene and medical science when we implore His assistance. By the way, how would Christian Science cure a case of smallpox or diphtheria? Would the 'healer' actually visit the patient? Wouldn't he rather demonstrate over him by telephone or give him what you call 'the absent treatment?'"

At this juncture Paxton awoke rather suddenly and rising to stretch himself poked his clenched fist into the Bostonian's face, causing that worthy gentleman to emit a yell of distress altogether incompatible with the tenets of Christian Science.

"A thousand pardons," exclaimed Paxton.

While struggling bravely to conquer the painful delusion of mortal mind the Bostonian asked: "If Christian Science be false, how do you account for its phenomenal success?"

"Our Lord accounted for it," replied Fr. Michaels, "when He said: 'There shall arise false Christs and false prophets and shall show great signs and wonders, in so much as to deceive (if possible) even the elect.' St. Paul also accounted for it in his second letter to Timothy, exhorting us to avoid those 'having the appearance, indeed, of godliness, but denying the power thereof. For of these sort are they who creep into houses, and lead captive, silly women laden with sins, who are led away with divers desires: Ever learning and never attaining to a knowledge of the truth.'"

CHAPTER XVII

CONFESSION

"Hola! Der Herr Professor!" exclaimed Mr. Grebma, by way of greeting to Doctor Wolfgang, whose annual attack of hay-fever had driven him to the Island for a two weeks' sojourn.

"I am so glad you came," said Mr. Grebma, shaking him warmly by the hand. "Shortly before leaving on his vacation Fr. Michaels imposed a convert for instruction on Mrs. Grebma, who claims that her pupil asks more questions in a minute than an ordinary Christian can answer in a month. Here they are now!" As he spoke, Mrs. Grebma and Miss Seymour alighted from a carriage and proceeded leisurely up the walk.

"Welcome to Mackinac," exclaimed Mrs. Grebma, pantingly, as she reached the veranda and fanned herself vigorously. Then scrutinizing the thermometer, she continued: "Mercy! If it is 89 degrees here, what must the poor people have to endure in Chicago!" After going through the formalities of an introduction the party sat down. "Take this chair, Father," said Mrs. Grebma, "it is more comfortable. Miss Seymour was remarking as we came up the walk, that it must be dreadful to tell our sins to a priest. I replied that it wasn't any harder than taking calomel, quinine or cod liver oil."

"Very true," commented Dr. Wolfgang. "Nobody is fond of medicine, and yet we all prefer the physician's visit to that of the undertaker. God doesn't want confession to be pleasant, otherwise relapsing into sin would become too easy. How delightfully simple it would be for the sinner to say under his breath: 'O Lord, I stole $100.00; I burned down my store in order to get the insurance; I have ruined my neighbor's reputation; I am living in the proximate occasion of sin.' It becomes more difficult when such a person is told by the confessor: 'Before you can receive absolution, you must restore the ill-gotten goods, repair the injury done, abandon the sinful occasion as far as it lies within your power.'"

"Well, I don't see," declared Miss Seymour, "why we can't confess to God alone, since He alone has power to forgive sin."

"Neither do I," replied Dr. Wolfgang, "unless it is because God has ordained otherwise. Hawthorne in the Marble Faun puts your objection into the mouth of his Puritan heroine Hilda after she had disclosed her secret to the English confessor in St. Peter's Basilica. The scribes made the same objection to our Lord: 'This man blasphemeth. Who can forgive sins but God only?' And yet is there anything to prevent God from delegating His power? He delegated men to promulgate His law. Why should He not authorize men to absolve us when we break it? Governments negotiate with each other through their ambassadors and God pursues a like method. In the present order of Providence we can find no other means of pardon outside of sacramental confession when the latter is available."

"Why," exclaimed Miss Seymour, "I was taught to regard confession as an invention of priestcraft for the purpose of keeping the people in ignorance and superstition."

"Strange," said Dr. Wolfgang, "that the cunning priests didn't exempt themselves from the onerous duty of confessing their sins. Did your teacher inform you of the precise epoch in which the celebrated invention occurred?"

"I think that it was in the XIII century," replied Miss Seymour.

"The IV Lateran Council held in the XIII century did not invent confession," said the doctor, "but presupposing its existence, specified when the faithful should confess their sins. As well might the County Collector be accused of having invented taxes when he notifies us that they should be paid on or before May 1st. It may surprise you to learn that confession was not only foreshadowed but even divinely commanded centuries before Christ raised it to the dignity of a sacrament. Under the Mosaic Law the Jews were bound both to confess their sins and to offer atonement sacrifices according to the measure and estimation of the sins. How could the Jewish priests proportion the victims to the number and quality of the offenses, unless the people were obliged to confess their sins in particular?

"Our Lord, having made St. Peter visible head of His Church, said to him: 'I give to thee the keys of the kingdom of heaven. Whatsoever thou shalt bind upon earth shall be bound in heaven and whatsoever thou shalt loose upon earth shall be loosed in heaven.' This implies the power of loosing and binding the spiritual bonds of sin. The same power was afterward conferred upon the other Apostles. 'Breathing upon them, He said: 'Receive ye the Holy Ghost, whose sins you shall forgive they are forgiven them, whose sins you shall retain they are retained.' He made the Apostles judges of human souls on earth, so that absolution granted or denied by them is a true sentence ratified by Him in heaven. If we could obtain pardon independently of the tribunal established by Christ, it would become nugatory and useless just the same as our criminal court if law-breakers were not subject to its jurisdiction."

"How do you prove," asked Miss Seymour, "that priests to-day have power to forgive sins?"

"Every institution of Christ destined for the general welfare of the Church," replied the doctor, "must remain in full force and vigor as long as the Church lasts. When our Lord said to the Apostles: 'Going therefore teach all nations . . . baptizing them,' etc., He certainly did not restrict the power of preaching and baptizing to the Apostles alone. He meant that those prerogatives should be exercised by their successors until the end of time. Hence by a just parity of reasoning the words: 'Whose sins you shall forgive,' etc., must extend to their legitimate successors in the apostolic ministry, viz.: to the bishops and priests of the Catholic Church. They exercise this power by hearing the confession of sins and by forgiving them, not as private individuals, but as ministers of God and in His name."

"It must be very humiliating to tell every little secret fault to the priest," remarked Miss Seymour.

"Why," rejoined the doctor, "we needn't tell the little ones. It is only the big ones, the mortal sins that we are bound to confess. If we deliberately conceal a mortal sin, our confession is thereby rendered worthless and sacrilegious. In that case not only must we declare the sin concealed, but repeat all the grievous ones committed since our last worthy confession. It would be like a mistake made in fastening our clothes or shoes. It doesn't suffice to undo one button. We have to unbutton them all and start over again properly from the beginning. Of course, it is humiliating, but that is one of the essential features of a worthy confession. We must accuse ourselves with a deep sense of shame and sorrow, truthfully and honestly, without excuse or exaggeration, at the same time indicating to the best of our memory the number and kinds of our mortal sins and the circumstances changing their nature."

"Why should one go into so much detail?" asked Miss Seymour.

"Because," said the doctor, "the confessor is our judge and spiritual guide. What kind of a sentence could he pronounce without hearing the evidence or merits of the case? Do you think that a patient would convalesce, were the physician to prescribe for him without diagnosing his malady beforehand? If the penitent does not confess all the mortal sins of which he is conscious according to their number and kind, the confessor cannot prudently judge whether to grant or deny absolution; he cannot impose a penance proportioned to the offenses; nor can he prescribe suitable remedies enabling the unfortunate sinner to rise from spiritual death to the life of grace."

"But don't you think," asked Miss Seymour, "that God will forgive any sinner who reforms?"

"It all depends upon what you understand by reformation," replied the doctor. "An humble and contrite heart God will never despise. Three acts are required on the part of the sinner that he may be forgiven: contrition, confession and satisfaction. He must conceive an inward, supernatural and sovereign hatred of all his mortal sins, and a true grief of the soul for having offended God with a firm resolution to sin no more. He must confess all his mortal sins humbly and sincerely to a duly authorized priest. Finally he must be disposed to perform the penance enjoined by the priest."

"All aboard for the golf links!" shouted Mr. Grebma, from the rear porch.

"I am with you," responded Dr. Wolfgang, rising. "Will you kindly excuse me?" he added, turning to Miss Seymour.

"Oh, certainly," replied the latter.

"If you call here to-morrow morning at nine o'clock," said the clergyman, "I will be glad to resume the instruction."

CHAPTER XVIII

THE HOLY EUCHARIST

"Is there much difference between the Episcopalian and the Catholic Church?" asked Miss Seymour the next morning.

"All the difference in the world," replied Dr. Wolfgang. "The Episcopalian Church was founded by Henry VIII because Clement VII refused him a divorce from his lawful wife. The Catholic Church was established by Jesus Christ and has continued uninterruptedly down to the present day. The English Episcopalians recognize the reigning sovereign King George as their spiritual head. Catholics throughout Christendom regard the Sovereign Pontiff, Pius X, as the visible head of the Church and the Vicar of Christ upon earth."

"Well, the Episcopalians have the communion service just the same as Catholics," said Miss Seymour.

"Oh, no, they haven't," responded Dr. Wolfgang. "They have merely the shadow without the substance, the empty figure without the reality. In the days of Elizabeth they claimed that the Eucharist contained really and truly bread and really and truly the body of Christ."

"Isn't that what Catholics believe?" asked Miss Seymour.

"Catholics," replied the priest, "do not believe that a thing can both be and not be at the same time and under the same respect. Ours is a rational faith. If the Holy Eucharist is really bread, it cannot be the body of Christ. And if it is the body of Christ, it cannot be really bread. When the Anglicans finally awoke to the glaring absurdity of their doctrine, they took refuge in the figurative sense of Calvin, viz: this bread is a figure, a symbol; it represents my body. Just as when our Lord compared Himself figuratively to a vine, a door, a rock or a lamb."

"Well, that sounds more plausible," commented Miss Seymour.

"But it isn't more plausible," rejoined the priest. "Just because some Scriptural phrases are evidently metaphors, it doesn't follow that all Biblical expressions must be interpreted figuratively. What would become then of the Blessed Trinity, the Incarnation, the Redemption, Original Fall, Eternal Reward and chastisement? Why not consign these and other doctrines to the limbo of tropes and figures? Whenever our Lord employed figurative expressions He invariably showed from the drift of His conversation that they were figures. When He said: 'I am the vine, the door,' etc., the subject is the personal pronoun I which remains invariable and excludes all change in the Person of Christ. Hence those expressions are figurative, according to the common rules of speech. 'I am the living bread that came down from heaven,' is also a metaphor, and had our Lord said no more our Protestant friends might have had a little shading of grammar on their side. In speaking of the Holy Eucharist, He did not content Himself with saying: 'I am the living bread.' At the Last Supper, taking bread into His hands, He said: 'This is my body.' Lest we might dream of tropes or figures, He added: 'My body which shall be delivered for you.' Taking the chalice of wine, He said: 'Drink ye all of this. This is My blood which shall be shed for the remission of sins.' In the Syro-Chaldaic, Greek and Latin Text the subject is not the personal pronoun I which in the objected phrases would imply a metaphor. No, the subject is the demonstrative pronoun THIS without any other adjunct. The Latin Vulgate reads: Hoc est Corpus meum. Hoc viz. This, in the neuter gender referring to Corpus Body which is also neuter. It cannot refer to panis, viz: bread which is masculine. 'Unless you eat the flesh of Man and drink His blood,' said our Lord, 'you shall have no life in you.'"

"I was always taught," said Miss Seymour, "that our Lord wished us to eat His flesh by faith. That was simply a figure of speech."

"His hearers didn't understand it as a figure," said the priest. "They took His words literally. In fact they disputed among themselves saying: 'How can this man give us his flesh to eat?' Many of the disciples exclaimed: 'This is a hard saying, who can hear it?' What difficulty would they have to believe, if He merely wished them to eat a piece of bread to His memory? Do you know what the expression — 'to eat the flesh of another,' means when taken figuratively?"

"I do not," replied Miss Seymour.

"Well, in all oriental languages as well as in plain Anglo-Saxon," replied the priest, "it means to abuse, to calumniate, to backbite. Don't we say in English of an enemy: He nearly ate me alive; he almost devoured me? Hence the figurative sense of our Lord's words would be: Unless you abuse and calumniate the Son of Man, etc., an evident absurdity."

"I never knew exactly," said Miss Seymour, "what Catholics believe regarding the Holy Eucharist."

"They believe," said Dr. Wolfgang, "that in the Holy Eucharist not only is our Lord Jesus Christ really present, but also that the substance of the bread is changed into His body and the substance of the wine is changed into His blood while all the appearances of the bread and wine remain unchanged. That is what we understand by the term — transsubstantiation. At the Last Supper our Lord said: 'This is my body. This is my blood.' Those words in their plain and obvious meaning imply a change of substance. If that which our Saviour held in His hands was really His body, then it must have ceased to be substantially bread."

"How can it be the body of the Saviour, if all the appearances of bread remain?" asked Miss Seymour.

"That's the same old HOW of the incredulous Jews and disciples of little faith," replied Dr. Wolfgang. 'They disputed among themselves, saying: How can this man give us his flesh to eat?' Before seeking to understand how the Eucharistic bread and wine are changed into our Lord's Body and Blood, explain how He changed the water into wine at the marriage feast of Cana. How is the water of the raindrop changed every season into the wine of the grape? How is the food we daily consume changed into our flesh and blood?"

"But Father," insisted Miss Seymour, "in the natural phenomena quoted, not only the substance but also the appearances are completely changed, while in the Holy Eucharist the appearance of bread and wine remain."

"Very true," replied the priest, "I cited those examples as imperfectly illustrating the substantial change that occurs in the Holy Eucharist. But in petrification do not the appearances of wood, the shape, color, quantity, etc., remain invariable, though the wood itself is substantially changed into a mineral, a piece of stone?"

"But our Lord is one person," said Miss Seymour, "yet you claim that He is daily received by thousands or even millions of communicants."

"I presume," said Dr. Wolfgang, "that like most ladies, you rarely pass a looking glass without taking a furtive glance at your hat to see whether it is on straight?"

Miss Seymour nodded affirmatively.

"Well," continued the priest, "how is it that your reflection in the mirror would be multiplied as many times as the fragments into which the mirror might be broken? How do a thousand persons in the church receive whole and entire each word that falls from the lips of the preacher? If our Lord could miraculously multiply five loaves and two fishes so as to appease the hunger of a multitude in the desert, what is there to prevent Him from miraculously multiplying His sacred presence so as to give Himself as spiritual food for our souls in Holy Communion? Infidels think it absurd that our Lord, a full grown man, can be present in the small space of a consecrated host. Yet they cannot explain how a broad landscape stretching for miles along the horizon can be so accurately reflected in the tiny retina of the eye."

"But, Father," protested Miss Seymour, "surely we are permitted to believe our eyes."

"Certainly, and also your ears," rejoined the priest. "In fact you can attach belief to all your senses. What do your senses perceive in the Holy Eucharist? The sensible qualities of bread, viz.: its shape, taste, color and quantity. All those sensible qualities are so necessarily present, that when they disappear, the Body and Blood of Christ disappear along with them. In seeking truth we cannot depend upon the testimony of one organ of sense alone. The gift of sight after all conveys to us merely the appearance of things. You behold a person in the street and you take him for an old acquaintance. You run up and accost him. But no sooner does he speak than you discover your mistake. Did your eyes deceive you? No, they performed their office with integrity. They represented what certainly appeared like an old acquaintance and the wrong conclusion was in your judgment. Reason and experience testify that if we wish to know the true nature of objects, then in their investigation we must employ all our senses. In the example of the person whom we mistook for an old friend, the error was rectified by our sense of hearing. No sooner did we hear his voice, than we realized that he was a stranger. Let us do the same with the Blessed Sacrament. Our sight, taste, etc. represent it as bread. But what about our sense of hearing? Do we not hear the infallible voice of Jesus Christ exclaiming: 'This is My body; this is My blood'? Our hearing, therefore, conveys to us His Divine Word and prevents the wrong conclusion into which we would certainly fall, if we hearkened to the testimony of our other senses."

CHAPTER XIX

SYMBOLISM OF VESTMENTS AND CEREMONIES

"Have you ever assisted at Mass?" enquired Dr. Wolfgang of Miss Seymour, when she came for her usual morning instruction.

"Yes, indeed," she replied, "and I thought it very impressive."

"I hope that I am not intruding," said Mrs. Grebma, as she approached with some needlework in her hand, and sat down upon the veranda.

"Not at all, Madame," replied the priest. "The more, the merrier; the larger the audience, the better I like it. Do you wish to hear about the color and symbolism of the vestments worn by the priest when he says Mass?"

"Oh, yes," she answered, "kindly explain why different colors are used."

"Every woman," said the priest, "is or ought to be anxious to appear well gowned before her husband and friends. The Church being the Spouse of our Lord, likes to appear before Him in dress of pleasing and mysterious variety. Although her essential glory and beauty are from within, she gives them outward expression through the variously colored vestments employed in her ceremonies. White, a symbol of purity and sanctity, is used on feasts of our Lord, the Blessed Virgin, the Angels, Pontiffs, Confessors and Virgins. Red, suggesting the idea of blood and fire, is employed to celebrate the festivals of martyrs. Since it is the work of the Holy Ghost to enlighten our minds and inflame our hearts, and as He descended upon the Apostles in the form of fiery tongues, the color red is used also upon His festivals. Violet, a color partly dark and partly bright, recalls both the labors and advantages of mortification. Hence it is employed in the penitential seasons of Advent and Lent. Black, a symbol of mourning, is used on Good Friday and in Masses for the dead. Green, signifying hope, is employed on all ordinary Sundays and weekdays when no special feast occurs. Everything connected with the Mass suggests in some way the divine tragedy enacted on Mt. Calvary."

"What special meaning is attached to the vestments?" asked Miss Seymour.

"The first garment the priest puts on," said the doctor, "is the amice which means to cover. It is a square white cloth fastened with two strings crossing each other on his breast. It symbolizes the veil with which our Savior was blindfolded when the rabble struck him saying: 'Prophesy to us O Christ who it was that struck thee.' It also typifies a warrior's helmet reminding the priest that he is a soldier of Jesus Christ. Putting it on he says: 'Place on my head, O Lord, the helmet of salvation that I may withstand the attacks of the devil.' The alb or long white linen robe recalls how our Savior was clothed in derision by Herod. Its whiteness implies the great purity which the priest should bring to the celebration of Mass. Donning it he says: 'Cleanse me, O Lord, and purify my heart, that having been made white in the blood of the lamb I may reap eternal joys.' Not only Christian but also Jewish and Pagan priests have always employed linen tunics in their ceremonies. The Jewish high-priest was clothed with it for sacrifice. The pagans were similarly vested when immolating victims to their deities. The idea was stolen from the Mosaic ceremonial. Man, it seems, was always conscious of his fall. He knew that vestments made from the coverings of animals were not pure enough. So he laid them aside and donned linen when engaged in religious functions. The cincture recalls how our Lord was bound with cords in the Garden of Olives, when scourged at the pillar, and finally when ascending Calvary. The cincture holds up the alb which might inconvenience the priest in walking. It warns him that his virtue should be strong and energetic, that in order to ascend the altar and drink the blood of the Immaculate Lamb he should renounce all worldliness. Hence in girding himself he says: ' Encircle me, O Lord, with the girdle of purity and extinguish within me all tendency to sensuality, so that I may preserve intact the fairest of virtues.' The maniple was formerly a kind of handkerchief used to wipe away tears and perspiration. It recalls that we must earn the bread of immortality by the sweat of our brow and that our Lord will wipe away all tears and misery when we appear before His tribunal to receive our recompense. Placing it upon his left arm the priest says: ' May I deserve, O Lord, to carry the maniple of grief and pain that I may receive in joy the reward of labor.' The stole placed around the priest's neck and extending to his knees is a symbol of dignity and authority. He wears it whenever administering a sacrament. It also typifies immortality, the right to which we lost through the sin of Adam. Putting on the stole the priest says: ' Restore to me, O Lord, the robe of immortality which I lost by the sin of my first parent, and though unworthy I approach thy sacred mysteries, grant that I may attain eternal happiness.' The chasuble, the last vestment, was formerly a very large round cloak without any openings in the sides. The Greek Church still preserves it in its original form. During the last few centuries the Latin Church has gradually removed from it whatever interfered with the freedom of the arms. In its ancient shape it was lifted up whenever the priest had to use incense or elevate the sacred Host or Chalice. Notwithstanding its present shape the custom of holding up the chasuble on these occasions is still retained as a memorial of by-gone days. It symbolizes the yoke of our Lord which priest and people should daily carry. This yoke is the observance of His law. Putting on the chasuble the priest says: ' O Lord, Who has declared: My yoke is sweet and my burden light, grant that I may carry it in such a manner as to obtain Thy grace.' A large cross is drawn on the chasuble that we may have continually before our eyes the obligation to carry the cross after our Savior, and may remember that this symbol of our redemption is our only hope, that the altar is a true Calvary where the sacrifice of the cross is renewed and perpetuated.'"

"I heard," said Miss Seymour, "that every movement of the priest at the altar has a special significance."

"It has," replied Dr. Wolfgang. "The celebrant proceeding with the acolytes to the sanctuary represents our Lord going with His disciples to the Garden of Olives. The profound inclination made during the Confiteor recalls the Savior's agony when He fell prostrate to the ground. The priest kissing the altar reminds us of how our Lord was betrayed by Judas into the hands of His enemies. When from the middle of the altar he goes to the Epistle side and from the Epistle returning to the center to pass over to the Gospel side and back again to the center, he represents Jesus led first to Annas and Caiphas who judged Him guilty of death; then brought before Pilate who declared Him innocent, and from Pilate to Herod who clothed Him as a mock king and sent Him back to Pilate's tribunal where He was condemned to be crucified."

"During these ceremonies," asked Mrs. Grebma, "should we not meditate upon our Savior's passion?"

"Certainly," rejoined the priest, "since the Mass is a memorial of His passion. The Gospel and Credo remind us that we must stand up for our faith and courageously profess it whenever duty requires. The removal of the veil from the chalice suggests how our Lord was stripped of His garments when scourged at the pillar. The oblation of the host and chalice recalls how our Savior offered the chalice of His bitter Passion to His heavenly Father for the sins of the world. The priest washing his hands at the Lavabo reminds us how Pilate did likewise before the people saying: 'I am innocent of the blood of the just man.' The Orate Fratres or Pray Brethren recalls the admonition of our Lord to the slumbering Apostles: 'Watch and pray lest ye enter into temptation.' The consecration, the most solemn part of the Mass, vividly recalls the scene of the Last Supper when our Lord changed the bread and wine into His adorable Body and Blood, and empowered His Apostles and their successors, the bishops and priests, to do the same, exclaiming: 'This do ye for a commemoration of me.' The elevation of the consecrated Host and Chalice reminds us how our Divine Redeemer was raised upon the cross for the salvation of mankind. The priest continues to pray, and our Lord while hanging from that infamous gibbet continued to intercede for His executioners, exclaiming: 'Father, forgive them for they know not what they do.' The division of the Host typifies the death of our Savior, who expired, saying: 'Father, into Thy hands I commend my spirit.' A particle of the divided Host is let fall into the chalice to symbolize the soul of Christ descending into Limbo. At the Agnus Dei the priest strikes his breast, thus recalling how many of those witnessing our Savior's death struck their breasts, exclaiming: 'Indeed this was the Son of God.' Communicating the priest buries as it were in his heart the Body and Blood of Christ. Joseph of Arimathea, Nicodemus and others placed the lifeless Body of our Lord in the sepulchre. Towards the end of the sacrifice the priest, turning toward the congregation, says: 'Dominus Vobiscum — The Lord be with you.' It is our risen Savior announcing peace to His Apostles in the cenacle. Finally he blesses the people and leaves the altar, like our divine Redeemer blessing the Apostles before His ascension into heaven."

CHAPTER XX

CREMATION

After running the gauntlet of porters, cabmen and idlers who swarmed about the dock, Fr. Michaels managed to wedge his way through the dense crowd and cross the Rush Street bridge. Unused to the confusion and bustle of city life, more than once he narrowly averted being run down by passing vehicles. Tightly gripping his suitcase, he proceeded west at a lively gait on River Street, to Wabash Avenue, where he came in sight of the Loop. Scurrying across the street he collided with a cross-eyed man, who angrily demanded why he didn't look where he was going. "And why don't you go where you are looking?" retorted the priest, as soon as he had recovered his breath from the impact. He finally reached the Elevated Station and boarded a Metropolitan train that brought him to within a few minutes' walk of the house of Fr. Nathan, a former classmate. The greeting was most cordial and Fr. Nathan did all in his power to render the sojourn of his guest agreeable. The daytime was spent in sightseeing, visiting the parks, churches, and public buildings.

"One thing you must see before leaving town," said Fr. Nathan.

"What is it?" asked Fr. Michaels.

"The Marquette Building," replied Fr. Nathan. "The relief work in the rotunda is really artistic. It is a mosaic sketch of Fr. Marquette's life and labors among the Indians."

"Well, I have had enough for one day," said Fr. Michaels, yawning. "We can take it in to-morrow." That night he was awakened by a furious ringing of the front door bell. A few minutes later Fr. Nathan knocked at his door.

"I am very sorry to disturb you," he said, "but I left my ritual and oil-stock in your room."

"What's the matter, a sick call?" asked Fr. Michaels.

"Yes, and a very urgent one," replied the pastor. "Some unfortunate cut up by the cars." Whereupon he hurried down stairs and left the house. Fr. Michaels said a decade of his beads for the poor victim and was soon fast asleep.

"Did you reach him in time?" he asked of Fr. Nathan at the breakfast table the next morning.

"Oh, yes," replied the latter. "A couple of brakemen came after me and I rode back with them on a switch engine. I had to bring along a candle and a bottle of holy water, as they never have anything prepared in that hospital. The surgeon was very deferential. He and the nurse withdrew while I was hearing the poor fellow's confession. I dared not give him the Viaticum as he could retain nothing. He only lived a couple of hours and was conscious up to the moment of his death. Although mashed across the abdomen he never uttered a moan or whimper. He was stretched on the operating table when I entered and he recognized me immediately. 'I got mine all right, Father,' he said. 'I had it coming to me.' Here is an account of it in the paper."

Fr. Michaels took up the paper and read:

> VICTIM OF RAILROAD CROSSING
>
> "George Paxton, a traveling salesman, aged 30, while crossing the C. M. & St. P. R. R. tracks, stepped out of the way of the Limited directly in the path of a train of Pullman cars that were being switched on a siding. Several of the cars passed over his body before the accident was discovered. He was taken to the Emergency Hospital where his case was pronounced hopeless."

Fr. Michaels was stunned. "The Lord have mercy on his soul," he exclaimed. "Paxton was on the boat with me."

He then briefly related the circumstances of their first meeting.

"He and his mother," said Fr. Nathan, "have lived in the parish a long time. She always practiced her religion, but he was rather wild and careless. I expect to have trouble over the funeral. She will want him buried in Rose Hill alongside of his father, who wasn't much of anything from a religious standpoint. He desired to be cremated, but she would not consent to that."

"His burning desire may have been gratified when he reached the other side," commented Fr. Michaels. "To consign the remains of a cherished relative or friend to the devouring flames of a crematory recalls vividly to mind the infernal abode of the reprobate who on the last day shall hear that awful sentence: 'Depart from me ye cursed into everlasting fire prepared for the devil and his angels.' The Church has always shown the greatest respect for the mortal remains of her children, at the same time avoiding the excesses of paganism. That is why she abolished the barbarous custom of burning the dead."

"I don't see any opposition to Catholic doctrine in the practice of cremation," remarked Fr. Nathan. "It prevents corruption of the soil, contamination of the air and drinking water, and is really a safeguard against infection in time of cholera and yellow fever."

"You are evidently trying to start an argument," responded Fr. Michaels smiling. "In every well regulated cemetery the coffins are placed at least five or six feet below the surface. Decomposition of their contents is too far removed from corn and wheat fields, rivers and fountains, to cause either corruption of the soil or contamination of the drinking water. You know as well as I that the practice of cremating bodies obtained official recognition in Europe through Masonic influence. It is in full accord with the maxims of atheism, the chief aim of which is to banish God from the birth, nuptials, and death of mankind. All nations, even the most barbarous, guided by the light of natural reason, have understood that the Divinity should intervene in these three solemn events of human life. Christians invite God to be present at the birth of their offspring in order to regenerate them in the salutary waters of baptism, make them His adopted children and heirs to the kingdom of heaven; they ask Him to preside at their nuptials, because the married couple has special need of divine assistance to persevere in conjugal fidelity and to educate their children in a Christian manner, that they may eventually become useful members of society; finally they invoke His presence when death approaches, to prepare them for their journey into eternity. All such considerations are scorned and ridiculed by infidels, who boast of depriving their children of baptism, who substitute a civil contract for the religious ceremony of marriage, who on their deathbed repulse the ministrations of a priest and finally desecrate death itself by making provision in their wills for the cremation of their bodies. It is the final act of the atheist in defiance of Christ and His Church. The pagans used to throw the bodies of the martyred Christians into the flames and vainly imagined that the resurrection of their bodies was thereby rendered impossible. Of course in time of war or pestilence, when neither time nor opportunity allows corpses to be buried, and delay were a menace to the living, then in the interests of public safety, the Church permits cremation. But under ordinary circumstances she wants her children to receive the benefit of the Requiem Mass with all the prayers of her ritual. She desires their remains to be buried in consecrated ground under the shadow of the cross."

"Of course Catholics as a general rule," said Fr. Nathan, "must be buried in a Catholic cemetery, but didn't the Baltimore Council make an exception in favor of converts?"

"Yes," replied Fr. Michaels, "in favor of converts whose surviving relatives have a family lot in a non-Catholic graveyard, and also in favor of Catholics who, in good faith, acquired title to such a lot before or even after the promulgation of the decree in 1853 forbidding them. Outside of these cases no priest is allowed to conduct the funeral services of the faithful buried in a non-Catholic cemetery without the permission of the bishop."

"I have often wondered," said Fr. Nathan, "why the Church is so rigorous in forbidding the interment of non-Catholics in our cemeteries. Refusal seems rather cruel, especially in the case of unbaptized infants, mixed marriages, etc. We had just such a case here a few months ago. The Bishop granted permission, but insisted upon the casket being bricked up and separated from the other graves."

"The relatives could not blame you," replied Fr. Michaels. "Burial in a Catholic cemetery is regarded as a kind of communion. According to Leo the Great, we cannot hold communion in death with those who in life were not in communion with us. The funeral rites of the Church constitute a mark of respect which is not to be shown to those who in their lives have proved themselves unworthy of it. The Roman ritual, vi, c. ii, denies Christian burial to Pagans, Jews and infidels; to heretics and their adherents; to apostates, schismatics and persons excommunicated by name or placed under an interdict; to suicides who have taken their lives through desperation or anger (excepting the insane), or unless before death they showed signs of repentance; to those killed in a duel even though repenting before death; notorious sinners who die impenitent; those who have not received the sacraments of confession and Communion once a year during the Easter time and have expired without any sign of sorrow; unbaptized infants and those having made provision for the cremation of their bodies after death."

"Oh, had Paxton not received the last sacraments," exclaimed Fr. Nathan, "I would certainly decline to officiate in any capacity at the funeral and forbid his remains to be brought to the church."

"Poor Paxton hadn't the remotest notion of dying when I parted with him last Monday," said Fr. Michaels. "Who does ever think of it? Preparation for death should be our chief occupation in life. Although no other affair can be more lamentable in its failure, yet how little concerned we are about preparing for eternity! We can talk glibly enough about trifles pertaining to our honor, interest or amusement, but the theme of death is invariably banished from our conversation."

"You can talk about it at the funeral if you like," said Fr. Nathan. "Why not remain over and preach the sermon?"

"Thanks," replied Fr. Michaels, "but I am due in Pittsburg Friday. If I were to preach, it would not be a eulogy on poor Paxton, who only furnished young men with an example of what they should avoid. I don't believe in flattering panegyrics that do not help the departed, and merely furnish the surviving relatives with ammunition for their vanity. What I shall do, is to call upon the grief-stricken mother before my departure."

And he kept his word. For the next day he visited the heartbroken woman and tried his best to console her. He realized how little any expression of condolence could avail in her bereavement. "The case would have been far worse," he said, "if her boy had been killed instantly."

She brightened up when he told her how her son had called upon him at the rectory and spoke of his mother in terms the most affectionate.

"Why, what could have induced him to visit you, Father?" she asked, the tears glistening in her eyes. "If he saw Fr. Nathan approaching the front door, he usually disappeared through the kitchen."

Would he tell her how her unfortunate boy had contemplated marrying a divorced woman? Perish the thought. She had already sorrow enough. "Oh, he came to me for spiritual advice," he replied. That was indeed no lie.

CHAPTER XXI

PREDESTINATION

Fr. Michaels boarded the Pennsylvania Limited which left the Chicago Union Depot precisely at 3:00 P. M. Shortly after the train passed Englewood a porter entered the smoking compartment. He unlocked several doors, made a few dabs with a dust rag at the faucets and basins and finally laid out an array of small towels for the benefit of those inclined to lave themselves of Chicago's dirt and smoke.

"Does this train stop at Valparaiso?" asked a portly passenger who was pulling vigorously at a Bridgeport panatella.

"No, sah," retorted the knight of the whisk broom, with something akin to indignation in his tone. "Dis heah train don't eben hesitate at Valparaiso. It only stops at Fote Wayne befoh it reaches Pittsburg at midnight." After a while most of the smokers retired, leaving the compartment in possession of the portly gentleman and Fr. Michaels.

"Getting off at Pittsburg?" he asked of the clergyman.

"Yes, sir," replied the latter.

"Well, you are going to a mighty dirty town. I have always regarded it as a pocket edition of Chicago. Pittsburg has one advantage, though, over Chicago; its streets are always clean after a rain, because they all run down hill."

"Perhaps that accounts for the downward pace of some of its millionaires," remarked Fr. Michaels.

"Maybe," laughed the portly gentleman; then scrutinizing the Roman collar, he added: "I would size you up for a preacher."

"I am afraid that you might change your mind if you ever heard me," replied the latter.

"Ah, I knew that I could not be mistaken," said the portly gentleman, complacently. "Are you an Episcopalian?"

"No, sir, I am a Catholic priest from Mackinac Island, Michigan."

"You don't say! I spent a week up there last summer at the Grand, and I never met so many gentlemen of the Jewry before in all my life. They are about the only ones who can afford to stop there. Delightful spot, isn't it? I enjoyed rambling through those groves of pine and balsam. Your people have the finest church on the island."

"It is a fine church for a small place," said Fr. Michaels, "but rather a lonesome one in winter."

"I am not much of a church-goer," said the portly passenger. "It has been a case of bread and butter with me since I left school. I really never had any time for religion. I always try to treat everybody on the square. The Lord decided our fate before we were born. He knows whether I shall be saved or lost in the shuffle. Hence it would do me no good to worry about it."

"First call for dinner!" shouted a white-aproned waiter as he passed the doorway.

"That sounds good to me," said the portly gentleman. "Come out and watch me turn the bill of fare into a hungry man."

"What is the use of worrying about dinner?" said the priest. "I can't understand why you worked so hard or what induced you to take this train for Pittsburg. Why didn't you leave all these things to God who knew from eternity whether you would realize them or not?"

"Leave your grandmother," exclaimed the portly gentleman. "I have inside information that it is time to eat. I haven't had a bite since breakfast, but have been racing around tending to business until train time."

"You certainly ought to do as much for the business of your eternal salvation," said the priest. "Why not give it serious thought, as if it all depended upon you? Were you ever in the Board of Trade?"

"Yes, and to judge from the antics of those brokers, one might imagine that they had broken loose from an asylum."

"Your seeing them interfered in no way with their liberty of action, did it?" asked the priest.

"Why, no."

"Well," continued the priest, "God knows all past, present and future events down to their minutest details. He leaves us free to do and say what we please according to the liberty He has given us. We do things, not because He sees them, but He sees them because we do them. His knowledge of our actions in no way hampers our freedom. If we observe His law and abstain from sin, or if we truly repent of sin committed, He sees that we will be saved. If we sin grievously and persevere in it unrepentant until death, He foresees that we shall be lost. His infinite knowledge is like the mirror in the panel of that door in which all our movements, even the most insignificant, are most accurately reflected. On what depends that one gesture rather than another is portrayed in that glass? On our individual liberty. Man is like an actor on the stage. What does the audience perceive? Just what the actor does and nothing more. Although God knows perfectly well before the curtain rises just what the drama will be, yet it will not differ from what the actor intends to make it. A while ago you said: 'God knows whether I shall be saved or lost.' You wished to thereby convey that if you are predestined, you shall be saved; and if not predestined, no matter what you may do, you shall be lost. That is the heresy of Calvin, claiming that God created some to be saved and others to be damned, irrespective of their merits or demerits. Now, what has God done in predestination? He has sanctioned with His decree what He has foreseen you to freely determine. If God has foreseen that, by abusing your freedom and His grace, you will continue in sin until death, He has decreed that you shall be lost. His foreknowledge, however, is not the cause of these events happening, but He foresees them because they shall occur. Predestination is not the cause of your doing good or evil and thus saving or losing your soul;

but the fact of your choosing a wicked or virtuous life is really why God sees you from all eternity among the reprobate or elect."

"But then," said the portly gentleman, "I don't see how God's decree regarding my salvation can be infallible, if I am free to adopt my own mode of living."

"Your objection," said Fr. Michaels, "cannot be urged against your salvation any more than against the recuperation of your health, the gaining of a victory or any other event foreseen by God as depending upon your free will. All these natural events, though known by God from eternity, we firmly believe to depend upon our efforts. Hence to regain health we submit to medical treatment; to sustain life we eat, and to conquer we fight. So it is in the supernatural order; although God wishes all men to be saved, yet we firmly believe that it depends upon their coöperation. Hence they must pray, avoid temptation and observe His law. Just as you would reasonably ascribe the loss of health, fortune and life to the negligence of the person ignoring the necessary means to preserve these things, and not to the fact of their having been foreknown by God, so the loss of salvation should be attributed to the criminal negligence of the unfortunate sinner refusing to employ the necessary means to obtain it. When God decreed our restoration to health, the preservation of our life and fortune, it was because He foresaw that we would employ efficacious remedies, avoid dissipation, practice economy, etc. Likewise when He predestined us for eternal happiness or misery, it was because He foresaw that we would adopt or discard the means of salvation."

CHAPTER XXII

EXISTENCE OF HELL

"You surely don't believe," said the portly gentleman, "that an all merciful God will condemn anyone to the eternal pains of hell, do you?"

"I certainly do," said Fr. Michaels, "just as I believe that an all just God will reward the good with the eternal joys of heaven. God is not only merciful, He is also just. His mercy cannot be foolishly exaggerated to the exclusion of His justice. He is good, and for that reason He sent His only begotten Son into the world to redeem it by His passion and death upon the cross. According to St. Paul, He wishes all men to be saved and to come to a knowledge of the truth. Hence He affords us all sufficient grace to attain salvation. He is all merciful and forgives us after we have grievously offended Him, provided we repent. But on the other hand His infinite mercy doesn't blind Him, doesn't render Him stupid or an accomplice of our iniquities. Although infinitely good, the Bible assures us that He created a place of neverending torment for the rebellious angels with whom thieves, drunkards, adulterers and other transgressors of His law shall be associated. Notwithstanding His infinite mercy He destroys peoples and nations when the measure of their crimes is filled up. He often strikes down the obdurate sinner in the midst of his iniquity. The same merciful Redeemer who forgave Mary Magdalen, the woman taken in adultery, and the repentant thief on the cross, has also solemnly declared: 'You shall seek me, but you shall not find me, and you shall die in your sin.' We Catholics believe in the eternal pains of hell just as firmly as in the everlasting joys of heaven, and as much as in the infinite perfections of God Himself."

"No one ever came back from hell to tell us about it," said the portly gentleman.

"Very true," replied Fr. Michaels. "Those having the misfortune to go there are not supplied with return tickets. Belief in eternal punishments and rewards for man after death is as old as the world and as widespread as the human race. This conviction is so thoroughly implanted in the human conscience that we find it among all nations ancient and modern, civilized and barbarian. It forms a part of nearly every creed. The Universalists are about the only sect daring to repudiate it. By so doing they brazenly contradict the plain assertions of Him, who on fifteen different occasions, speaks in His Gospel of "everlasting punishment," "unquenchable, inextinguishable fire." Whom are we to believe? Short-sighted sentimentalists who do not know what they are talking about, or Him who is the way, the truth and the life? What audacity that man with his puny reason should presume to fathom the inscrutable decrees of God Who can neither deceive nor be deceived!"

"Well, I don't pretend to know much about His decrees," said the portly passenger, "but just the same it would take a good deal of reasoning to persuade me that God is going to send anyone to hell."

"Why?" asked the priest.

"Because God would be guilty of revenging Himself, and revenge doesn't harmonize very well with the spirit of Christianity."

"Indeed," said the priest. "Then we miserable creatures can insult and outrage His infinite majesty as we please, and God is powerless to command our respect! Think of what you say when you attribute revenge to the Deity. We mortals are not allowed to take revenge for many reasons. In the first place because we can never fully know the extent of guilt our offending neighbor has in his heart which is seen by God alone. We are forbidden to take revenge because it implies an act of authority which one individual cannot exercise over another for the simple reason that he doesn't possess it. We are not allowed to take revenge because passion usually blinds our judgment whenever our personal interests are involved. It is forbidden us because God wishes us to imitate the meekness and charity of Christ. For these and many other reasons revenge becomes in us a transgression. But in God, the Supreme Lord and Master, the case is altogether different. Sin is a most grave disorder, for it violates His eternal law, and it must be repaired. When sinful man does not repair the offense by voluntary expiation it must be repaired by compulsory reparation, and God being the author of all order attends to it personally. In Him is perfect knowledge of the fault and all its circumstances. Hence He can exact reparation with perfect justice. In Him is supreme authority. Therefore He only exercises His right. In Him there is not, nor can there be blindness of passion. Consequently He judges with perfect equanimity. He punishes the fault because both its deformity and His infinite justice demand it. According to our feeble mode of expression we call divine vengeance what is simply an act of supreme justice rectifying the evil of sin with the good of the punishment. Don't delude yourself with the idea that God is only good and merciful, for it may expose you to the danger of finding Him only just. There are two kinds of sinners who ought to take this into serious consideration. Those continually presuming on His infinite mercy. Let them realize that His very mercy compels Him to punish them, lest there be established in the world the vicious principle that the more merciful He is, the greater the liberty of offending Him with impunity. The other class is composed of those continually vilifying and persecuting the good, because they suffer in patience. Of course the latter cannot, must not, seek revenge during the present time of probation. But a day will come when, free from human passions and through pure zeal of justice, they will cry to heaven for vengeance, and God, Who reserves to Himself the right of revenge, will hear their prayer. He shall then render it clear to everyone that His goodness does not prevent Him from punishing crime, and that to take revenge for the offenses committed against His holy law is not incompatible with His infinite justice."

"Do you believe," asked the portly passenger, "that devils armed with pitchforks are incessantly prodding the reprobates in a pool of fire and brimstone?"

"The pitchforks and brimstone," rejoined Fr. Michaels, "are figments of the imagination. Catholic faith teaches that the pains of hell are eternal and of a twofold nature — the pain of loss and the pain of sense. The first consists in the privation of the beatific vision, the loss of God the greatest good which alone can satiate the longings of the human soul. The continual consciousness of this irreparable loss causes the reprobate unutterable anguish. The indescribable torment of sense is produced by a real, material, inextinguishable fire which differs from ordinary fire, as it doesn't need to be replenished with fuel in order to continue burning."

"I hate to think of it," said the portly gentleman.

"It isn't a cheerful topic," commented the priest, "any more than the penitentiary, the noose or the electric chair. If people meditated more on hell, they would hesitate before offending God."

"Well, Father, I have enjoyed the talk just the same," said the portly gentleman. "Won't you join me at dinner?"

"Thank you very much," replied the priest. "I dined very heartily before boarding the train. I will recite my breviary while you are at table. If you like, we may resume our conversation upon your return."

CHAPTER XXIII

CAPITAL PUNISHMENT

"Father," asked the portly gentleman upon his return from the dining car, "what do you think of capital punishment?"

"In certain cases I think it necessary," replied the priest. "I don't believe in public executions nor in lurid descriptions of them by the newspapers."

"I have always regarded capital punishment," said the robust passenger, "as a legal assassination. If I were on a jury trying a man for murder, I would certainly not vote to hang him."

"Well," rejoined the priest, "to consider capital punishment as a legal assassination implies that it is unnatural, intrinsically evil, and consequently in no time, place or circumstance lawful. Anyone familiar with the Bible knows that in the Old Law the Jewish priests and people were divinely commanded to punish certain crimes with death. Evidently then in the sight of God there are transgressions for which capital punishment is not excessive. Among all nations and in all ages it has been inflicted for certain crimes. Do you think that the whole human race has agreed upon making assassination a law? Of course anarchists, assassins and burglars are unanimously against it for obvious reasons."

"Well," retorted the fat man with a little warmth, "I am neither an anarchist, assassin, nor burglar, and I am against it. The object of punishment is to reform the culprit and make of him a better citizen. How will you accomplish that by electrocuting or stringing him up?"

"If the sole end of justice," replied the priest, "were the reformation of the guilty, your objection might have some weight. But penalties are needed for restoring order and protecting society. For most murderers capital punishment has been a signal blessing. It has been the sole means of making them prepare for eternity. After sentence has been pronounced and the day of their execution appointed, they begin to realize the enormity of their crime and return to God by a sincere repentance. Usually the only reformed murderer is the one executed. Of course there are other ways of converting him besides putting him to death. The state cares for its citizens collectively and for the individual citizen only in his collective aspect. It never hangs a man for his own good, but for the good of the community. In many instances the extreme penalty is necessary, if we wish to have any semblance of proportion between the crime and its punishment. In how many cases have we felt that hanging was altogether too mild a chastisement? Finally it is necessary for the protection of society. Violated rights must be vindicated and ample protection must be given against future attack. While the former may be obtained by condemning the culprit to hard labor for life, the only efficacious remedy for protecting the lives of the citizens is by putting murderers out of existence. Their execution has a salutary influence upon others murderously inclined."

"But life imprisonment would bring about that result," said the portly gentleman.

"Hardly," replied the priest. "If fear of death itself is unable to deter certain criminals, the terrors of a life sentence will have little effect upon them. Rarely will you find a culprit condemned to life imprisonment who doesn't entertain the hope of being eventually liberated before the expiration of his sentence, either through executive clemency or flight."

"Well, no man," said the portly passenger, "has the right to take away the life of his fellowman, and the commandment: 'Thou shalt not kill,' is binding upon the State just as much as upon the individuals composing it."

"The power of inflicting capital punishment, like the power of levying taxes and enforcing laws for its preservation, is inherent in the State, not in the individual," replied Fr. Michaels. "While in self-defense man is justified in killing his fellowman, he can never do so as an act of retributive justice which would be usurping the State's prerogatives."

"That sounds like state absolutism," said the stout gentleman. "You evidently believe in the 'divine right of kings.'"

"Not at all," rejoined Fr. Michaels. "That was the pet theory of the so-called reformers. Henry VIII and James I of England claimed the plenitude of both spiritual and civil authority, to such a degree that it could never slip away from them or their descendants. When James I mounted the throne of England and proclaimed that 'God appointed the king absolute master, and all privileges which co-legislative bodies enjoy, are pure concessions proceeding from the king's bounty,' a cowardly parliament swallowed this bitter pill of absolutism without a murmur. But when a court preacher embodied the same sentiment in a flattering discourse before Philip II of Catholic Spain, do you know what happened? The populace denounced him to the Inquisition, and the unfortunate man was not only severely reprimanded, but obliged to retract his words in presence of the king. We Catholics believe that all authority, whether of monarchy or republic, is neither from king nor people, but from God. We recognize the civil authorities as His representatives, and, as such, render them obedience."

"You don't believe, then, in the sovereignty of the people, or in letting the people rule?" asked the portly gentleman.

"No, I don't believe in the senseless political twaddle uttered by demagogues to catch the popular vote. How can the people give what they do not possess? Authority alone is the basis of all rule and legislation. By authority we mean the power of defining rights and obligations, rewarding observers and punishing transgressors of its precepts. No man can be at the same time his own legislator and subject. Conscience therefore must be the interpreter of some authority superior to the individual. It must reëcho the voice of the Supreme Legislator. The natural sense of right and wrong revealed to each one through the dictates of conscience must be identical with the eternal law. The same principle applies to individuals when united in civil society. The binding power of human legislation consists in enforcing the natural law, in applying the eternal principles of equity and justice. If the civil power enacts unjust measures and consequently opposed to the eternal law, the fountain head of all legislation, there is no obligation to observe them. Because civil law can only oblige in so far as it is an expression of the Divine Will. Hence the Apostles refused to obey the civil authority forbidding them to preach in the name of Jesus. They followed the injunction of our Divine Redeemer: 'Render unto Cæsar the things that are Cæsar's, and unto God the things that are God's.' Such has ever been the doctrine theoretically and practically advocated by the Catholic Church. Despotism has never found a shelter within her fold. Read the history of her struggles throughout the ages, and you will find that they were invariably with tyrannical rulers and not with their unfortunate subjects. When the so-called sovereign people are permitted to rule, what happens? In applying the law to transgressors, there is never question of reforming or life imprisonment. Without preliminary trial or review of evidence they resort to mob violence which speedily terminates in a lynching bee or burning at the stake. On account of the barbarous excesses of the Sovereign People wreaking vengeance upon supposed law-breakers, the State of Colorado restored capital punishment in 1901, although four years previously it had been erased from the statute books. Capital punishment then is not a legal assassination and to assert that civil authority has not the right to inflict it for certain offenses is to ignore the A-B-C of jurisprudence. It is only when men begin to seek the kingdom of heaven rather than the gratification of their passions that the need of capital punishment will cease to exist.

CHAPTER XXIV

NECESSITY OF RELIGION

"Father," said the portly gentleman, "I don't think heaven so hard to reach as you priests imagine. I rarely see the inside of a church, unless it be to attend a wedding or funeral. We don't have to enter a church in order to pray, do we?"

"Very true," replied Fr. Michaels, "God can hear our prayers wherever we happen to be. Yet those wishing to be heard when they address a king, usually go to his court and present themselves in the proper place of audience. Now the church is the proper place of audience of the Great King of kings. Although He can hear the voice of man everywhere, still it was expedient that certain places should be set apart and dedicated to His honor above all others, in order to awaken reverence in men and encourage them when they offered their petitions. 'My house shall be called a house of prayer.' God has a special connection with the temples erected for divine worship under his direction and inspiration. In the universe He is seen as the Almighty Creator and Ruler, but in the church He is manifested as the Savior of men. In the works of creation He gives us the natural revelations of Himself, but in the church we have His Gospel revelations. We Catholics frequent the church in order to assist at the Holy Sacrifice of the Mass, receive the sacraments and hear the word of God."

"But what is the use of all these rites and ceremonies? I worship God in my heart and that ought to suffice."

"Well, my robust friend," said the priest, "let us briefly analyze your so-called religion of the heart and see if it be really enough. Man is a creature composed of a soul and body. The soul taken alone is a separated spirit; the body without the soul is a corpse. To form a living man they must be united. In consequence of this union how does man act? His every act is a combined operation proceeding from soul and body. Just try to feel some sentiment in your soul without giving it outward manifestation. You turn pale with fear, red with anger and green with envy. Your face becomes radiant with joy, depressed with sorrow, and if desperately in love the symptoms may be recognized a block away. If this be the case with our ordinary actions, why shouldn't it be so in our exercise of religion? How would you define religion?"

"I wouldn't," replied the fat man, slightly coloring at his embarrassment.

"Religion," continued the priest, "is a virtue obliging man to render due homage to the Creator. Even if man were able to worship God solely in his heart, it would not suffice. Why? Because religion is a duty incumbent not only upon the individual man, but also upon society. The people must take part in it. If each man is absolutely dependent on God and morally obliged to acknowledge that dependence by some outward act of recognition, a similar duty obliges the whole human society which is but an organized multitude of men. Society depends upon God just as much as the individuals composing it. Hence we Catholics have the Holy Sacrifice of the Mass which is a public act of worship offered by the priest for society, for the people. Were the President to visit Chicago, would the patriotic citizens content themselves with honoring him privately in their hearts? Hardly. You would see public buildings and residences gorgeously decorated and no end of receptions and banquets arranged in his honor. Now God is Supreme Lord and Master not only of individuals, but also of society. Therefore society is bound to recognize and adore Him by public acts of religious worship. Can its members unite in purely mental acts like the angels without any external communication? This may be characteristic of those practicing "religion of the heart," but we poor mortals cannot have religion of the heart without revealing it through the senses. Have you any special time set apart for practicing this marvelous cult? Do you really enter within yourself occasionally and humbly ask God's pardon for your sins, at the same time firmly resolving to offend Him no more? At stated intervals do you actually offer Him the worship of that great heart of yours which, you claim, is the only incense that should burn upon the altar of the Divinity? Or isn't it rather a subterfuge, because you realize that total absence of religion might place you before the world on a level with the brute? To profess any religion would be equivalent to assuming its obligations, and that you do not wish to do. Hence you have recourse to an invisible religion, viz: that of the heart. Thus you avoid the stigma of being considered irreligious, at the same time ignoring all religious duties. It is certainly a wonderful invention, for one may claim to cultivate religion of the heart while leading the life of a pagan! The only drawback is that while hoodwinking the world, it is impossible to deceive God Who sees the inmost recesses of the heart."

"That may be all very true," said the portly gentleman, "but I am still waiting for you to show me what need God has of your rites and ceremonies or what advantage He derives from your bowing and scraping in the churches."

"Why," replied Fr. Michaels, "God has no need of our prayers nor does He derive any advantage from our ceremonies. The need and advantage are entirely on our side. Did you imagine for a moment that we base the necessity of religious worship on the indigence of the Creator? We are absolutely dependent upon Him, not He upon us. If He did not continually preserve us, we would lapse into our original nothingness. Do you see that beautiful moon shedding its silvery rays over the adjacent country? Let us imagine that the moon didn't wish to depend upon the sun on the pretext that the sun doesn't need it! It is not for the sun's good that the moon must depend, but for its own advantage, otherwise it would remain in perpetual darkness. The judge doesn't need the culprit, the rich do not need the poor, nor do the strong need the weak. God certainly doesn't need us miserable sinners, but we stand in constant need of His grace and mercy. Does the absence of need on the part of the creditor dispense his debtors from paying what they lawfully owe him? Almighty God has such an essential, absolute and inalienable right to our gratitude, worship and adoration, that He could not dispense us from these religious duties without ceasing to be God."

"But," retorted the portly gentleman, "did not the Savior expressly condemn external worship when He said to the Samaritan woman at the well: 'The hour cometh and now is when the true adorers shall adore the Father in spirit and in truth'?"

"No, He didn't," replied the priest, "otherwise He would have contradicted Himself when in the garden of Gethsemane He prostrated Himself in prayer to His eternal Father, or when He attended the sacrifices and other religious functions in the temple. Adoration in truth implies external worship. If you refuse externally with your body to adore God the Creator, Preserver and Benefactor of your body as well as of your soul, you cannot be rightfully called a true adorer. In the passage quoted our Lord wished to teach that the sacrifices of Jews and Samaritans were soon to be replaced by a true form of worship of which spiritual, interior feelings of reverence towards God and correct notions of Him would be the chief characteristics. He contrasts the true adorers with the Jews and Samaritans of that period, not with those who lived according to the spirit of the Law. The patriarchs and prophets certainly adored God in spirit and in truth, though they performed external acts of worship. They outwardly expressed what they inwardly felt."

CHAPTER XXV

GAMBLING

During the conversation of Fr. Michaels with his fellow passenger a trio of gentlemen were deeply absorbed in a game of poker at a table in a corner of the smoking compartment. "I don't suppose you sanction that kind of amusement," said the fat man, nodding his head in the direction of the players and slyly winking at one of them, a grizzled, bottle-scarred veteran. "The churches are opposed to popular amusements, Sunday baseball, cards, dancing, and the theater.

"What harm can there be for a crowd of men and boys to watch an interesting game of baseball on a Sunday afternoon?"

"No harm whatever," replied Fr. Michaels. "All week they are cooped up in factories, stores or offices. If Catholics comply with their religious duties by assisting at Mass Sunday morning, the Church does not object to their taking innocent recreation in the afternoon. It is far better for them to be out on the bleachers developing their lungs at the expense of umpire and players than to be squandering their week's wages in debauchery. A sound mind in a sound body is a blessing that we cannot long possess without occasional recreation. Amusements are therefore necessary. They are the orchestra accompanying us through life's drama, childhood, youth, manhood and old age. At death the curtain falls and rises in eternity, where we are rewarded or punished according as we have merited."

"Oh, I believe in plenty of outdoor exercise," said the fat man, thumping himself reproachfully upon the abdomen. "I know that I don't get enough of it."

"So say we all of us," ejaculated one of the players. "What have you got?"

"A pair of typewriters," responded the veteran.

"No good," exclaimed the first. "I have aces."

"In taking recreation," continued Fr. Michaels, "three things must be avoided. We must not seek enjoyment in things unlawful or injurious. Some amusements are essentially degrading and demoralizing, as e. g., cock-fights, dog-fights and prize-fights to a finish. No self-respecting person should encourage such spectacles by his presence. The ban should be placed on those slugging football games which require the services of an undertaker or at least a surgeon. The same may be said of the annual auto and motor cycle races, and the Marathon endurance tests, after which some of the participants are physical wrecks fit for the cemetery or asylum. The next thing to be avoided are scurrilous and profane remarks like the ones uttered by that fellow every time he pretends to fail in drawing to his hand. Our amusements should always be in keeping with the dignity of man and our respective state in life. No one takes offense at the laity attending a ball, a horse-race, or a theatre. But the presence of the clergy at such entertainments would occasion scandal. In the selection of their amusements they must be guided by the Apostolic injunction declaring that what is not expedient or edifying is not allowed. Amusements, finally, should be indulged in at the proper time and place, always in moderation and never interfering with duty, otherwise they become unlawful."

"Wouldn't you like to take a hand, Father?" asked one of the players. "I'll stake you for a dollar's worth of chips."

"Oh, no, thank you," replied the priest. "I seldom play cards in private and never in public."

"Fairy tales," hummed the veteran, who held his cards almost at arm's length, and yet it was never possible to see all five of them in spite of his apparent recklessness. "How would you play that hand?" he asked, exhibiting to the onlookers what resembled a flush of diamonds.

"Oh, that should be worth at least a white one," commented the fat man.

"Yes, and then some," retorted the veteran, shoving a blue chip to the center of the table. "I may as well let you fellows down easy, for you're both young and inexperienced."

"Sorry that I can't even see you," whined one.

"Nor I," chimed in the other, laying down a small pair.

Meanwhile the veteran raked in the pot on a bob-tailed flush, which he lost no time in shuffling with the rest of the pack. "That's where you showed good horse sense," he exclaimed. "You may not realize it, but you're saving money every minute. Seeing people is an expensive luxury and the one who calls usually loses."

"Do you think that honest?" whispered the fat man to the priest.

"Oh, bluff is a part of the game," replied the priest. "Such ruses are allowed, otherwise the players might fall asleep. It were dishonest if he marked the cards, had a few up his sleeve, dealt from the bottom of the deck, or saw the cards of the others in yonder mirror. He would then be bound in conscience to restore whatever he dishonestly won."

"Don't you regard gambling as a sin?" continued the fat man.

"Not any more than I regard drinking a sin," replied the priest. "The sin in both cases lies in the abuse. Gambling in the strict sense is risking a forfeit upon the result of a chance game. To this category belong shaking dice, flipping coins and all card games into which there may enter an element of skill as well as of chance. Billiards and baseball, checkers and chess are regarded as scientific games in which, however, good luck often plays an important part. Nothing betrays a man's character quicker than the way he plays a game. If he possess a proud, covetous and irascible disposition, it will speedily come to the surface. To play any lawful game in moderation for trivial stakes just to keep up the interest is not wrong. All our thoughts, words and actions, amusements as well as afflictions, should refer in a measure to our last end. 'Whether you eat or drink, or whatever else you do,' says the Apostle, ' do all to the glory of God.' He accepts the oblation of our most commonplace actions, such as our meals, recreations and our sleep, because they all enter into the order of His divine Providence. When amusements do not interfere, but help us rather in the attainment of our last end, they become a virtue. Wagering or betting is not considered gambling unless the stakes be high. Moral theology is silent as to what constitutes a high stake. It must be determined according to the relative financial standing of the players. In order that playing a game for stakes may be free from sin, the four following conditions are required: 1. The player must risk his own money or property and have the free disposal of it. 2. He must act freely and not be unjustly coerced. 3. There must be no fraud or cheating. The ordinary ruses of the game, however, are allowed. 4. The chances of winning should be as equally divided as possible. An expert should not be pitted against a tyro unless the latter be given a suitable handicap. With the observance of these conditions, and if the object of the game be honest, the contestants enter upon a valid contract. They are obliged to pay their debts of honor although they cannot be legally compelled to do so. Owing to the many scandals and abuses, public gambling has been made a statutory offense in most countries.

" Some persons are born with an hereditary tendency to gamble as well as to drink immoderately and their only salvation is total abstinence from both. I remember the case of a young man who called one day to take the pledge against gambling. He had contracted the habit of feeding fifteen or twenty dollars of his salary on pay day to a slot machine kept in a cigar store. To beat these gambling devices the player has about one chance in a million. This unfortunate man had fallen into the clutches of a loan shark, to whom he was paying a monthly interest of ten per cent. on two hundred dollars! How many gamble away in a single night more than they could honestly earn in a week or a month! The craze has unfortunately taken hold of our society women for whom there is no true home life with its sacred responsibilities. These votaries of the gay world regard children as a nuisance, and husbands simply as the providers of their pleasures, a happy convenience for furnishing the money necessary for their unlimited extravagance in dress, bridge whist, theater parties and receptions. Home for them means the retirement in which they rest between one round of dissipation and another, and in which, after having slept part of their fatigue away, they begin anew to powder and paint, frizzle and primp for the next social onslaught. I recall a rather pathetic case that happened only a few years ago. Several society dames were invited to a luncheon, the guest of honor being a member of the theatrical profession. After the repast a game of bridge was introduced by way of entertainment. When one of the ladies was about to depart, the hostess informed her that she owed the guest of honor some sixty dollars. Upon reaching home, she told her husband, who, infuriated, wrote Madame Hostess a sarcastic letter enclosing a check to cover not only the loss but also the price of the luncheon. The unfortunate lady suffered also the loss of her husband, from whom she was subsequently divorced.

"Playing games for money has a tendency to foment and develop all the baser instincts of human nature, especially greed and avarice. It soon becomes a passion hard to control. It may easily occasion waste of time and health, loss of friends and wealth. The joy of the winner usually depends upon the grief of the loser."

"Have you never heard of the cheerful loser?" asked the fat man.

"Oh, yes," replied the priest, "but I regard him as a myth. No sane man sincerely rejoices over his own defeat."

CHAPTER XXVI

DANCING

"From an esthetic standpoint," said the stout passenger, "there is no form of physical exercise that tends to give an easier grace and carriage to the movements of the body than dancing. Modern society regards it as an indispensable accomplishment. If a person is invited to a social gathering and doesn't know how to dance, he really feels out of place and must act as a wall flower. I think that the churches by their condemnation of dancing have lost all hold and influence upon our young people."

"I can only vouch for the attitude of the Catholic Church in regard to dancing," replied Fr. Michaels. "Certainly nothing is more natural than to dance. Surprise a child with a new toy and it will dance with delight. Even grown-up people are sometimes inclined to manifest feelings of unexpected pleasure in this manner. Mary, the sister of Moses, and David, the royal prophet, gave vent to their holy enthusiasm on certain occasions by dancing. Up to the middle of the last century religious dances were observed in some churches of Spain and Portugal. Dancing is not unlawful in itself if decently conducted and excluding all dangerous familiarity and impropriety. It is an act of joy and the outward manifestation of joy is not forbidden by any law. The great trouble with our young people, full of life and animal spirits, is that they are often tempted to make a toil of a pleasure to the serious neglect of duty; they are sometimes inclined to overstep the bounds of moderation and even propriety. Although innocent of itself and occasionally employed on religious festivals, dancing, like many other amusements, gradually became degraded through the passions. It proved one of the popular features of pagan worship. Heathen gods were honored by licentious dancing. The modern ballet appended to nearly every comic and grand opera, although generally attributed to the XVI century, is in reality traced back to the heathen pantomimes of ancient Greece and Rome. The chorus girls impersonating soldiers, knights, and other masculine characters are an abomination and a caricature of the original ballet. 'A woman,' says Deut. xxii, 5, 'shall not be clothed with man's apparel, neither shall man use woman's apparel, for he that doth these things is abominable before God.' In Eccl. ix, we are warned not to frequent the company of a dancer nor to hearken to her conversation, lest we perish by the force of her charms. In another passage, which might be truthfully applied to many fashionable dances of the present day, we read: 'Because the daughters of Sion are haughty and have walked with stretched out necks, and wanton glances of the eyes . . . and moved in a set pace, the Lord will cover them with shame and confusion.'"

"Oh, I have no use for those Oriental importations, Salome, danse du ventre, bear hug and turkey trot," said the fat man. "I think that the police ought to raid every joint where such dances are being conducted. But I don't see any harm in the ordinary round dance, the waltz, two-step, polka, etc. The Catholic Church has condemned round dancing."

"You cannot prove it by me and I certainly ought to know," replied Fr. Michaels. "The Baltimore Council doesn't even mention, much less condemn round dances. Pastors are exhorted to forbid their parishioners from assisting at immodest dances. In this category I would not hesitate to include masked balls and the ones you have just mentioned. We warn our people against Saturday night dances, which are no preparation for the Lord's Day. We caution parents to keep their children away from these public 'shindigs' with saloon attachments, which are often the theater of drunkenness, obscenity and even murder! I cannot understand what kind of a conscience parents have who allow their sons and daughters to frequent such places. They don't seem to realize that this criminal indifference loosens for their offspring every moral restraint, populates our city slums and Magdalen asylums."

"Oh, those dance-halls over saloons should not be tolerated," said the robust passenger, "and some of the amusement resorts are just as bad. I spent a couple of months in Italy a few years ago. I didn't see young boys and girls gadding about at night as you do here."

"Of course not," said Fr. Michaels. "The good old-fashioned Catholic custom invariably followed by all classes in continental Europe, viz., of sending along a chaperon with young people, is a prudent, laudable measure that should be just as rigidly observed in this country. Italian parents would not dream of letting their daughter go to an evening entertainment without there being three in the party, and the third person one in whom they have unbounded confidence. Human nature is the same everywhere and Americans with all their chivalry are tempted by the world, the flesh and the devil just as much as the rest of men."

"What do you think of these annual charity balls?" asked the fat man. "It cost me ten dollars for one last winter."

"Why, if that is all it cost, you may deem yourself lucky," replied the priest. "With the ladies the admission is the smallest item. They must reckon with the modiste, the florist and liveryman, who are really the beneficiaries of the so-called charity ball. Fashionable dances, to say the least, afford a powerful incentive to jealousy, envy, vanity and conceit. What feuds and wrangles have arisen from the formation of the various committees! Such a person was appointed, another was completely ignored, and then the slanderous gossip and recriminations begin in earnest. The ball is ostensibly for charity, but what an amount of uncharitableness it often engenders! How much valuable time is consumed in preparation for the ball. What a satisfaction for these poor creatures of fashion to read in next morning's paper a glowing account of the gowns and jewelry they wore. They forget that raiment, being one of the consequences of original sin, the person drawing vanity from gorgeousness of attire is like the invalid who would glory in the bandages covering his wounds. Of course, dancing is not sinful in itself. Nor is the abuse of a thing any argument against its proper use. Moralists, however, assert that owing to shamelessness of attire, the unbecoming freedom of manner and conversation, dancing may become a grievous sin. No self-respecting woman should parade her physical form around a ballroom in a scanty décolleté sheath gown. The modesty of these same people would receive such a startling shock were they suddenly confronted at home in a night gown, wrapper or kimono by their near acquaintances. What strange inconsistency! Why are they not ashamed to appear publicly before strangers in a ball costume, which is infinitely worse? They may try to justify themselves on the plea that it is customary and fashionable. But our Lord calls them to an observance of Christian decency and not to a servile following of the fashion. The wearers of the hobble skirt, peek-a-boo waist and other indecent costumes wantonly exhibiting the outline of their figure are a menace to public morals. There is nothing in their appearance to distinguish them from the denizens of the underworld. The modern female raiment, or rather lack of it, is largely responsible for the insults to which women are nowadays subjected in our parks and thoroughfares. Let them dress properly and they will not be molested."

CHAPTER XXVII

THE THEATER

"I think," said the fat passenger, "that the theater causes about as much damage to morals as any other agency."

"The pulpit, press and theater are the principal factors in the formation of public opinion," replied Fr. Michaels. "The journalist and actor have an audience every day, in fact sometimes twice a day, the moving-picture show about ten times a day, while the preacher reaches his congregation about once a week. The theater reflects rather than causes popular sentiment. It certainly wields a great influence either for good or evil. The idiotic mannerisms and vices of society may be ridiculed out of existence by the withering arrows of wit and sarcasm hurled against them from the footlights. Stage enthusiasts, after witnessing plays like 'Ben-Hur,' 'The Sign of the Cross,' or 'The Christian,' are inclined to style the theater 'a school of morals.' It might be, were all performances as free from censure as the ones mentioned. Unfortunately, it is oftener a school of scandal. People do not frequent the theater to be morally instructed. Their object is relaxation, amusement, instruction in the graces of dramatic art and literature. Managers understand this perfectly. They realize that financial success depends upon the way in which they cater to popular sentiment. Hence they are constantly feeling the public pulse in order to ascertain what is for the moment popular and then reëcho it in their theatrical productions. Being adept in the art of cajoling popular passions, the theater can become the vehicle of immeasurable evil. Before the fall of the Roman Empire the barbarous scenes of the amphitheater and the frenzied excitement of the circus contributed perhaps more than anything else to the general corruption of the populace."

"Well, the Church," said the fat man, "certainly did a great work in abolishing those demoralizing spectacles."

"Yes," continued the priest, "she replaced them with religious dramas and tragedies drawn principally from the liturgy, Scripture and Christian martyrology. Much dramatic element is contained in our liturgy. While the Biblical passages recited by the priest in religious functions may be regarded as the epic feature, the lyrical part is found in the anthems and responses chanted by the choir. During the office of Tenebrae in Holy Week a triangular candelabrum containing fifteen candles is placed in the sanctuary. The top candle of white wax represents our Lord. At the end of the Benedictus it is hidden behind the altar and afterwards brought back to symbolize His death, burial and resurrection. The extinction of the other candles typifies the flight of the Apostles. The noise made by the slamming of books at the end of the Office represents the tumultuous advance and overthrow of the cohort led by the treacherous Judas into the Garden of Olives. Apart from the consecration, which is essentially the same sacrifice as that of the cross, what are the ceremonies of the Mass but a most dramatic representation of the circumstances attending the divine tragedy of Calvary! In the Old Testament what strong themes for tragedy are furnished by the books of Judith, Job and Ruth! Where will you find more dramatic types of heroism if not in the exemplary lives of the Christian saints and martyrs?"

"I would like to have taken in the Passion Play at Oberammergau during my trip to Europe," said the stout passenger, "but my time was too short and I had to get back. I saw 'Everyman' at Steinway Hall a few years ago and enjoyed it very much. Such plays do a lot of good."

"They," said Fr. Michaels, "are a remnant of the mediæval religious drama, which was divided into three classes: mysteries, miracles and moralities. Mysteries were concerned principally with the mystery of man's redemption accomplished through our Lord's Incarnation, Death and Resurrection. They introduced patriarchal tableaux, e. g., Abraham sacrificing his only son Isaac, and various other Messianic prophecies confirming our Savior's mission. Miracle plays dealt with marvelous incidents taken from the lives of the saints and martyrs. It is amazing what scenic effects and optic delusions were accomplished in those days when mechanical stage contrivances were in their infancy. Moralities taught moral truths allegorically through the personification of the various virtues and vices. The seven capital sins with their opposite virtues usually formed the dramatis personæ. Gluttony, e. g., is invited out to dine by Banquet. Afterwards he falls into the very disagreeable company of Colic, Gout and Dropsy. The moralities were gradually emancipated from church influence and became more and more profane. The Troubadours kept increasing the comic element until immoralities would have been a more fitting title for those productions. The Herods, Judases, devils and vices soon gained greater popularity among the rabble than the saints, martyrs and personified virtues. Magistrates, bishops and even popes were insultingly travestied in farces and comedies. License finally reached its limit and evoked the most drastic measures on the part of the civil authorities."

"The civil power ought to adopt a more stringent policy to-day in regard to some of the plays," commented the fat man.

"Yes, indeed," rejoined Fr. Michaels. "Some of the modern shows are remarkably bad, either on account of the things acted or recited, or owing to the indecent costumes in which shameless individuals have the brazen effrontery to appear. There are plays in which religion, the sacraments, especially matrimony, and all that we Catholics hold sacred, are exposed to raillery and contempt. In the cheap resorts and even in the more pretentious theaters scurrility is occasionally mistaken for wit and vulgarity for dramatic art. So fond has the public become of novelty that the Thespian profession is now open to the pugilist, bigamist, burglar, and in fact to any mountebank who has gained notoriety. Special plays with realistic scenes of prize-fights, the cracking of safes, etc., are composed to suit the special talent of these creatures who ought to avoid rather than court public gaze. Yet they pose as heroes and are starred throughout the country. Is there anything better adapted to demoralize the rising generation? Why, take even the standard operas. Can you mention a single one the plot of which is not based upon moral obliquity? According to all accounts the innuendo in one part of 'The Jewels of the Madonna' is so lecherous that the actors and actresses daring to produce it should be given a jail sentence as well as a heavy fine. For us Catholics the same rules in regard to dancing apply also to the theater. A play bad in itself, furnishing the proximate occasion of sin, must be avoided. 'Let pastors,' says the II Plen. Balt. Council, 'prudently admonish the faithful to avoid theatres and dramatic plays which they know to be bad and full of danger. Let them, however, be careful, lest following too rigorous opinions they restrict the liberty of the Gospel. Because the laity may assist at plays in which there is neither scandal nor the danger of sin.'

"The plays of Shakespeare, Tennyson and other reputable authors contain nothing as a general rule detrimental to faith or morals. Parents should ascertain the nature of the performance before allowing their children to witness it. This knowledge should be derived from prudent, competent persons. They may keep informed regarding the moral standard of plays through the daily press in which a special column is devoted to music and the drama. Catholics wishing to conform to the spirit of the Church do not frequent the opera or the theater during Lent, Advent or any Sunday throughout the year."

CHAPTER XXVIII

WOMAN SUFFRAGE

"What is the Church's attitude in regard to woman's rights?" asked the portly gentleman.

"The same as that of the American Constitution," replied Fr. Michaels. "She has the inalienable right to life, liberty and the pursuit of happiness. We place her upon an equality with man as far as the means of personal sanctification are concerned. In the Catholic Church 'there is neither male nor female. For you are all one in Christ Jesus' (Gal. iii, 28)."

"But as to voting, don't you place her on a level with idiots and criminals?" demanded the fat man.

"Why, no," rejoined Fr. Michaels, "the vast majority of prelates and priests would place her in the same category with United States soldiers and sailors, who in certain states are excluded from voting. Would you say that the defenders of our country are on that account placed on a level with the criminal class?"

"Well, I think," said the portly gentleman, "that just as the Renaissance period discovered men, so the present progressive age discovered women."

"Oh, pshaw," exclaimed the priest, "woman was discovered centuries before the present epoch. Why, she was very much in evidence in the Garden of Eden."

"I believe," said the fat man, "that the Bible story of Mother Eve's disobedience is responsible for nine-tenths of the prejudice existing against women to-day."

"I do not share in your belief," commented Fr. Michaels. "The Pagan nations lacked the story of her part in the downfall of the human race, yet they invariably treated woman as the vilest of creatures. The Japanese will not allow her to even pray. She is simply permitted to sigh and grunt while man engages in prayer. Jews and Christians who possess the Biblical narrative of the Original Fall have invariably treated woman with the greatest respect. Patriarchs and prophets unite in proclaiming her excellence. Where will you find eulogies greater than those recorded in the Old Testament of Judith and Esther, Miriam and Ruth? Read the praises of the valiant woman in the book of Proverbs (xxxi). Rachel, Rebecca, and Sarah are presented to the Christian bride as models worthy of imitation. Catholic liturgy has enshrined their names and virtues in the benediction and prayers of the nuptial mass. Eve's part in the Human Fall has certainly not prejudiced us against woman, for Catholic theology regards her guilt as insignificant when compared to that of Adam. He was the head of the human race and therefore chiefly responsible for original sin and all its dire consequences. The introduction of sin into this vale of tears is invariably attributed to Adam, and not to Eve. 'Wherefore as by one man sin entered into the world' . . . Whatever share Eve had in our guilt was more than counterbalanced by the part the Blessed Virgin had in our redemption."

"The last century has produced some wonderful types of womanhood," said the fat man. "Madame de Staël, George Sand and George Eliot have certainly attained prominence in the literary field. Then in religion we have Mrs. Eddy, Madame Blavatsky and the Fox Sisters."

"The novel writers mentioned were indeed clever," replied the priest. "As to the foundress of Christian Science, the expounder of theosophy and the promoters of spiritualism, I regard them as the rarest specimens of feminine humbug that the nineteenth century has produced. They devoted their time and talent to leading people astray. What benefit did these female mountebanks render mankind when compared with St. Catherine of Egypt, patroness of theologians, polemists, pulpit orators and philosophers? Your feminine romanticists should not be mentioned in the same breath with St. Elizabeth, Queen of Portugal, who founded hospitals and asylums for every human ailment throughout her kingdom. In this progressive age we hear of sentimentalists erecting infirmaries for lame cats and dogs! Consider the long list of Christian virgins, widows and martyrs, foundresses of religious orders conspicuous for their erudition, piety and self-abnegation. Why, in presence of this galaxy of heroines our social uplifters and advocates of woman's rights dwindle into obscurity."

"Do you ever allow women to preach in your churches?" asked the fat man.

"No," replied Fr. Michaels, smiling. "Our Catholic women must do their preaching chiefly by example. 'Let women keep silence in the churches,' says St. Paul, 'for it is not permitted them to speak, but to be subject. . . . If they would learn anything, let them ask their husbands at home. . . . It is a shame for a woman to speak in the church' (I Cor. xiv)."

"St. Paul should not have placed an embargo on women preachers," remarked the portly passenger, "as most of them are endowed with the gift of tongue."

"The Apostle," replied Fr. Michaels, "forbade them to teach or to use authority over man, as that would invert the order established by the Creator. 'Thou shalt be under thy husband's power and he shall have dominion over thee' (Gen. iii, 16)."

"The English suffragettes do not seem to recognize the power or dominion of husbands," said the fat man.

"Evidently not," rejoined the priest. "Think of the lives endangered by their fiendish attempt to burn the Dublin theater, in which the Prime Minister appeared. Destroying property and assaulting members of parliament with an axe will hardly advance the cause of woman suffrage. The British Government applied the proper remedy by inflicting a sentence of five years' penal servitude upon each of those female nuisances. They are a disgrace to their sex."

"What do you think the cause of this agitation among the women?" asked the fat man.

"Socialism is back of the entire movement," replied the priest. "To be convinced of it, you need but read the pamphlets issued by the Illinois Anti-Woman Suffrage Association, of which Mrs. C. F. Corbin is the president. Like Eliza Allen Starr, she is a convert from Unitarianism, and her essays upon socialism as it regards the status of woman are the most scholarly that I have ever read. She proves conclusively that woman suffrage is the cornerstone of socialism. The monthly organ of the Church League of Woman's Suffrage in London recently had an article on 'Freedom and the Vote,' strongly advocating certain practices which are subject to criminal prosecution in every civilized country of the globe. The suffragette pamphlets scattered throughout London are résumés of ingeniously perverted physiology, pathology and sociology purporting to scientifically demonstrate the inferiority and vileness of man. The general trend of this Satanic, socialistic literature is to induce mankind to adopt canine ethics in regard to matrimony, and to look upon monogamous marriage as a mere conventionality that should be speedily supplanted by free love, the only panacea insuring permanent peace between the sexes!"

"Oh," exclaimed the fat man, "our American suffragettes do not sanction such bestial views. I really do not think it a square deal to deprive women of their natural right to vote."

"My dear sir," responded the priest, "suffrage, whether for man or woman, is not a natural, personal right."

"What is it, then?" asked the fat man.

"It is a civic, territorial right, which the State can grant or deny as it deems best for the common good. Universal suffrage often proves more of a curse than a blessing to a community. What benefit, do you think, accrues to the State through the vote of vagabonds colonized in lodging houses a month before election by disreputable politicians? What is there to prevent women from being colonized in a similar manner in case they were enfranchised? It is simply a question of political expediency whether the public weal demands the extension of suffrage to women."

"Well, I think that it does," replied the fat man, "for it would strengthen the hands of those endeavoring to deal efficiently with such evils as the white slave traffic."

"Nonsense," exclaimed the priest, "if women only remained in their proper sphere, i. e., in the home circle, discharging faithfully the domestic duties which God has placed upon them, and for which nature has preëminently fitted them, instead of usurping the places of men in factories, stores and offices, the social evils would be greatly diminished. If our women become politicians and begin to gad about electioneering, who will tend to the training and education of the children? I am most emphatically against woman suffrage, not because I deem her man's inferior intellectually, but because the family, and the important domestic duties incumbent upon wives, mothers and daughters are doomed to neglect when she enters the political arena."

"Don't you think that woman suffrage would have a refining influence upon politics generally?" asked the fat man.

"I do not," retorted the priest. "The very fact of her being physically weaker than man would diminish her moral independence. Unable to cope with him, she would naturally have recourse to all the blandishments, coquetry, cunning and intrigue of her sex, thus introducing into the political contest an additional element of moral corruption. We have occasionally observed feminine tactics in electing officers of their organizations, and in duplicity, wire-pulling and general crookedness woman has mere man immeasurably surpassed. From the female politician may Heaven graciously protect us."

"Want to be brushed off, sah?" asked the porter.

"No," growled the robust gentleman. "I prefer to get off in the usual way. Well, here we are in Pittsburg," he said, turning to the priest and extending his hand. "If I run up to Mackinac next season, I may pay you a visit."

"You shall be always welcome," replied Fr. Michaels. "Meanwhile, if you give me your address, I will take the liberty of sending you a few Catholic books, the perusal of which may tend to bring you into the fold."

CHAPTER XXIX

CATHOLIC PRIESTHOOD

The morning after his arrival in Pittsburg Fr. Michaels repaired to St. Vincent's Abbey where he assisted at the ordination of a young Benedictine. A few days later the newly ordained priest celebrated his first Mass on which occasion Fr. Michaels spoke in part as follows:

"If in a priest's life there be any special time of jubilation, it must be when he is privileged to celebrate for the first time the Holy Sacrifice of the Mass. 'No act,' says St. Thomas, 'is greater than the consecration of the body of Christ.' It is the most solemn act of our holy religion. It is showing the death of the Lord until He come and the application of His infinite merits to our souls. It is executing the divine injunction: 'Do this in commemoration of me,' and fulfilling in part the prophecy of Malachy: 'In every place there is sacrifice and there is offered to my name a clean oblation.'

"Assuredly the present occasion must be one of joy not only for the young celebrant, but also for those related to him by ties of kindred and friendship. How consoling for them the reflection that they now have one of their own daily pleading for them before the throne of infinite mercy! The world, however, does not realize the value of the priesthood. Some are inclined to argue against the church from the imperfections of its ministers. They forget that God appointed men and not angels as the heralds of His gospel. For, as the Apostle explains, 'they can condole with those who are in ignorance and error because they themselves are compassed with infirmity.' Hence at the oblation of the host the priest says: 'Accept, Almighty Father . . . this immaculate host which I, Thy unworthy servant, offer up to Thee . . . for my many sins, offenses and negligences.' Priests then, are human, and in every age and nation they have the infirmities of human nature. Whether the priest be curate, pastor, prelate or pontiff, he never perfectly realizes the sacerdotal type, for that type is the God-man. Although the best of clergymen are poor imitations of their divine prototype Jesus Christ, yet in learning and virtue they as a body rise far above the average of men. It is much easier to attain perfection in the professional or commercial world than in the priesthood, for a perfect priest means another Christ, another God-man. The sacerdotal vocation is consequently as far above human professions as heaven is above earth. The priesthood is from God, a heavenly treasure deposited in fragile vases. The vase may be unworthy, but the value of the treasure depends not upon that of the vase. But are not a great many worthless vases? Are there not a great many wicked priests? No, the number is relatively small. Wasn't there a Balaam among the prophets? a Caiphas among the high-priests? a Judas among the twelve Apostles? If, unfortunately, there may appear at great intervals in the sanctuary, a wolf in sheep's clothing, thank God we have an overwhelmingly large number of good priests who are a credit to themselves, an honor to the church and to religion.

" People do not always appreciate the sacrifice and labor of the priest. He abandons the comforts of home, perhaps also the emoluments and glory of a brilliant career in the world in order to work for your salvation. The Church imposes upon him a life of celibacy that he may serve God with less restraint and with undivided heart. 'I would have you to be without solicitude,' says St. Paul. 'He that is without a wife is solicitous for the things that belong to the Lord, how he may please God.' He is daily engaged in offering prayer and sacrifice for the people, in preaching and exhorting, in administering the sacraments. Why should not the people in turn pray for him, lest perchance, after he has preached to others, he himself become a castaway?

" Abstracting from his human frailties, just think for a

moment of the awful power and dignity with which even the obscurest priest is invested — a power and dignity surpassing even that of the angels. For bear in mind that priests and not angels are the dispensers of God's sacred mysteries and the expounders of His law. To the priests and not to angels our Savior said: 'Do this in commemoration of me, thereby empowering them to change the bread and wine into His adorable Body and Blood. To priests and not to angels, He declared: 'Whose sins you shall forgive, they are forgiven them. Whose sins you shall retain, they are retained.' The priests are the physicians of the soul. 'Is there any man sick among you,' says St. James, 'let him call in the priests of the church and let them pray over him anointing him with oil in the name of the Lord, and the prayer of faith shall save the sick man; and the Lord shall raise him up; and if he be in sins, they shall be forgiven him.' The priest is the deputed instrument in the hands of God to minister to all our spiritual wants from the cradle to the grave. Scarcely are we ushered into this world than he pours upon us the salutary waters of regeneration making us God's adopted children and heirs to His heavenly kingdom. If we have the misfortune to forfeit God's friendship in the pursuit of the carnal pleasures and vanities of this world, it is the warning voice of the priest that awakens our conscience and recalls us to the path of duty. The absolution of the priest restores us to God's grace and friendship in the tribunal of penance provided we approach it with the proper dispositions. He nourishes our soul with the Bread of angels in the Holy Eucharist. Finally when our course is run and the shadows of death are drawing near, it is the priest who visits us in our illness, strengthens us with the consolations of religion, and with the last sacraments fortifies us for our journey into eternity.

"The life of the true priest is a continual sacrifice whether it be spent in the exercise of parochial duties or in the monotonous function of professor in the class room. No matter what portion of the Lord's vineyard may be assigned to him for cultivation, he has his crosses and trials to bear. It is only

God's saving grace and his constant coöperation with it that will assure his faithful perseverance to the end.

"If it be deemed a privilege for an American citizen to represent his government at one of the foreign courts, how much greater the prerogative to represent the court of heaven among all nations of the earth! How much more exalted the honor to be ambassadors of Jesus Christ! 'We are ambassadors of Christ,' says St. Paul, 'Christ as it were exhorting by us.' The jurisdiction of earthly representatives is local, but the authority of God's ministers is universal. 'Go ye into the whole world and preach the gospel to every creature.' When the priest announces the gospel we know that he is vested with authority and we believe that we hear, as it were, from the tabernacle the voice of Him who declared: 'All power is given to me in heaven and on earth. As the Father hath sent me, I also send you. He that heareth you, heareth me. He that despiseth you, despiseth me.'

"Learn then to respect the dignity of the priest and to appreciate the good work he is called upon to perform in the exercise of his ministry. Let no person wantonly assail his character in your presence. For in proportion as his reputation is lessened in sight of the community, his influence for good is weakened. Respect the priest as the ambassador of your Divine Redeemer. Honor him as the minister of God, as a friend, as a father who has nothing so much at heart as your eternal welfare. Upon the spiritual interest he takes in those entrusted to him depends his own salvation.

"Finally, pray for your priests and especially for this young Benedictine Father who to-day celebrates his first Mass at which we deem it both an honor and a privilege to assist. Ask Almighty God to keep him ever faithful in the discharge of his duties and to crown his labors in the priestly ministry with success."

CHAPTER XXX

A CATHOLIC (?) SOCIALIST

The journey by rail from Pittsburg to Buffalo is 270 miles and takes about 7½ hours. For the first ten miles the scenery along the route is by no means entrancing. The monotony of belching chimneys is broken by occasional glimpses of the Allegheny river paralleling the railroad for quite a distance. The traveler breathes a sigh of relief when his train, after having passed scores of foundries and smelting works, finally emerges into the open country with its vine clad hills and azure sky, free from stifling smoke and noxious vapors. For a stretch of nearly one hundred miles pumping oil seems to be the main industry of the valley. At almost every mile an oil derrick may be noticed in operation. Fr. Michaels left Pittsburg on the afternoon train. He had the seat to himself for about an hour when he was obliged to share it with a passenger who boarded the car at Kittanning. The newcomer was not very attractive. Before sitting down he removed his coat and hat, exposing to view a rather unshapely head thickly covered with tawny hair which he wore a la pompadour. The most conspicuous thing about his apparel was a flaming red necktie that perfectly matched his blotched complexion. Fr. Michael was finishing compline and could not help observing how rudely his fellow passenger kept peering at the open breviary. At length unable longer to restrain his curiosity, the newcomer blurted out:

"Say, you're a priest, ain't you?"

"Yeh."

"A Catholic priest?"

"Uh huh," replied Fr. Michaels, evidently trying to discourage further conversation.

"I'm a Catholic too. Here's my card," continued the newcomer, presenting a small pasteboard bearing the inscription:

ALOYS BENGL

"I would have taken you for a socialist," said Fr. Michaels, glancing furtively at the red cravat.

"That's correct," said Mr. Bengl. "I'm a Catholic socialist. Our party has no more to do with religion than has tariff, free-trade, populism or prohibition. Socialism is an economic, bread and butter question."

"A Catholic socialist," replied Fr. Michaels, laughing, "is rather a curious combination. Someone has compared him to a guinea-pig which is neither a pig, nor does he come from Guinea."

"Evidently you know very little about socialism," rejoined Mr. Bengl, coloring. Then fishing forth a folded paper from his pistol pocket, he continued: "Here is our platform adopted by our National Convention held in Chicago in 1908. Kindly listen to this plank: 'The Socialist Party is primarily an economic and political movement. It is not concerned with matters of religious belief.'"

"I had the pleasure," said Fr. Michaels, "of listening, recently, to a very able address by Mr. David Goldstein who at one time was a most enthusiastic comrade and is now a most exemplary Catholic. In his lecture he explained how that wonderful plank after a most strenuous debate was inserted into the platform by a majority of one! Delegate Lewis did not consider religion a good campaign subject, and if mentioned at all it would be better to tell the truth than appear before the country as liars and hypocrites. Berger, Hunter and Hillquit, however, decided that the plank would be tempting bait for such men as you, a great vote catcher, and their view prevailed. Of course the comrades love Goldstein about as much as the devil does holy water. You ought to get his book: 'Socialism, the Nation of Fatherless Children.' It is an excellent up-to-date exposition of socialistic fallacies, and should be in the library of every patriotic American irrespective of creed. He proves most conclusively that socialism is fundamentally atheistic, that it regards the present marriage relation as a capitalistic institution and must eventually yield to the bestial doctrine of free love. The movement is not only anti-Christian, but also anti-American. Its leaders have repeatedly declared that the two curses of our country, capitalism and Christianity must go before socialism can triumph. The Lord forbid that we may ever see its scarlet emblem of harlotry and bloodshed waving over our glorious country."

"Oh, I know," said Mr. Bengl, "that there is quite a number of infidels among the socialists, just as you will find them in any political party. But to assert that socialism is anti-Christian because some of its advocates are so, is absurd. That would convict the two old parties. The father of Jeffersonian democracy was an infidel, in fact the only president thus far who was not a church member. Then there was Ingersoll and other agnostics among the Republicans."

"The Church," replied Fr. Michaels, "condemns socialism not precisely because 99 per cent of the comrades, according to Hillquit's admission, happen to be atheists, but because its fundamental teachings are diametrically opposed to the tenets of Christianity proclaiming the inviolable rights of private ownership, the sacredness of the marriage bond, the natural and primary rights of the parents to educate their children."

"All our poverty and misery," said Bengl, "arise from private ownership of property which should be confiscated and become the common property of all under State administration."

"A good deal of our economic misery," replied Fr. Michaels, "springs from shiftlessness and intemperance on the part of labor, greed and luxury on the part of capital, and lack of religion on the part of mankind in general. 'Seek ye first the kingdom of God and His justice and all these things shall be added unto you.' There is the solution proposed by our Divine Redeemer. It is the neglect of this important duty that causes all our trouble. If instead of squandering his wages in gambling and drink the workman purchases a homestead, that represents the sweat of his brow. What right has the State to take it away from him? The socialist remedy is worse than the disease. To be cured of a headache we need not undergo decapitation."

"God never gave the earth to a few individuals, but to the whole human race," rejoined Bengl. "He gave man dominion over the entire earth. He gave us collective ownership, the very foundation of socialism. Universal collective ownership and universal coöperation is our motto. On this platform we stand and defy refutation."

"True," said Fr. Michaels, "God gave mankind in general dominion over the whole earth and did not assign parts of it to individuals. As Leo XIII wisely indicated, God left the limits of private ownership to be fixed by private industry and by the laws of different races. Man must cultivate the soil before it produces; he must leave the impress of his own personality upon it by the sweat of his brow. When he buys a piece of land with his hard earned savings, that land becomes his wages in another form. To confiscate it would be stealing the fruits of his labor. Do you own any real estate, Mr. Bengl?"

"N-no, I don't," stammered Bengl.

"I never met a socialist who did," commented the priest. "Although that doesn't seem to hinder the comrades from owning several wives. That was a rather nasty case brought against National Secretary Barnes in Chicago. Of course the socialist wedding of Dr. Herron, former professor of the Chicago University is notorious. The real dyed-in-the-wool socialists regard God and His Church as their greatest enemy. He decreed for all time: 'Thou shalt not steal. Thou shalt not covet thy neighbor's wife, nor his house, nor his field . . . nor anything that is his.' In these commandments you have the condemnation of socialism that would fain right a wrong by committing a greater wrong. It would remove injustice by wholesale robbery. The amelioration of social conditions is to be found in the observance of Christian ethics and not in their violation. The comrades exhort us 'to leave heaven to the angels and sparrows,' and seek heaven on earth by the gratification of the passions. Christianity teaches the gospel of fraternal love, justice and domestic purity; socialism foments class hatred, theft and prostitution. Its great ambition is to control the organized labor movement. Wherever a strike occurs as e. g. in Lawrence, Mass., you will invariably find socialist agitators inciting the strikers to violence and destruction of property. Like the cuckoo the socialistic bird would lay its pestiferous eggs in a union incubator expecting organized labor to hatch them out. Fortunately the most of our labor leaders realize that their worthy cause has nothing to gain but everything to lose by the cancer of socialism."

"Don't you believe in municipal ownership?" asked Mr. Bengl.

"Yes, of certain public utilities," replied Fr. Michaels, "such as light, water, telegraph and transportation. To obviate strikes and the consequent inconvenience to the public, I believe that the government should establish a minimum wage to be augmented or modified periodically according as the cost of living increases or diminishes. Of course the comrades assure us that when the millennium of socialism arrives men, women and children will be perfect. As a writer tersely expressed it, 'when each one owns all, nobody steals; when all are comrades no one wrangles; when everyone has all he can drink, nobody gets drunk; when all women are common, no one commits adultery; when all are bosses, every man obeys; when every appetite is satisfied, all men are angels.' You cannot stand upon your socialistic platform, Mr. Bengl, and remain a Catholic."

"Why not?" asked the latter.

"Because," replied the priest, "it is morally rotten."

CHAPTER XXXI

VOCATION

Fr. Michaels left Buffalo Wednesday night at nine o'clock on the *Northland*. He retired early and arose the next morning before the boat reached Cleveland. The voyage on the Detroit and St. Clair Rivers winding in and out like a ribbon between verdure-clad shores reminded him of a trip on the Grand Canal of Venice. He could not help but notice the emphatic contrast between the American and Canadian banks, the former having decidedly the advantage with its hotels, summer cottages and well trimmed lawns stretching down to the water's edge. What a pity the tourist of meager purse could not subsist for at least a few days on sunshine and scenery. The attractive features of the trip were painfully marred by the war prices extorted for meals in the dining-room. It was with feelings of real joy that he landed the next day towards noon at Mackinac and proceeded to the rectory.

"Welcome home," said the housekeeper. "That convert has been calling up nearly every day since your departure to know when you would return. It would be a blessing if she left the island."

"Why?" asked Fr. Michaels.

"Because," replied the housekeeper, "she is causing too much gossip. Her frequent visits to the rectory have been noticed. Last Wednesday she tried to drown herself and it is rumored that somebody wrote to the bishop telling him that she tried to commit suicide on account of the priest!"

Fr. Michaels looked serious. "The bishop is a sensible man," he said at length. "If the writer signed his name, he will be given a chance to prove his assertion. If it is one of those cowardly, contemptible, anonymous communications, the bishop will consign it to the waste-basket. Tell me about her attempted suicide."

"Well," continued the housekeeper, "last Wednesday afternoon the Minchione boys were strolling along the beach near British Landing and saw her standing on the edge of the pier. They noticed her throw her handbag into the water. They started to run towards her, but while they were still a hundred feet away she calmly removed her hat, threw it after the pocket-book and plunged into the water. Both boys jumped after her and brought her ashore. Then one of them began a search for her pocket-book. Exhausted from her struggle and half fainting with excitement she pulled herself to her feet, exclaiming: 'Oh, please don't look for it; there's nothing in it of any value.' But Ralph managed to find it and gave it to her."

Just then the door-bell rang and the would-be suicide was ushered into the parlor. She looked ten years older. Fr. Michaels made no comment on her appearance.

"I had quite a lengthy interview with the Archbishop regarding your marriage," he said. "His Grace declared that if it be proven by documentary evidence that your former husband, John Betruger, was baptized, even though there remain some doubt as to the validity of his baptism, and it is certain that you were not baptized when you married him, then owing to the impediment — disparity of cult — your marriage can be pronounced null and void. If on the other hand, it can be shown that he was never baptized, or if nothing can be ascertained regarding the fact of his baptism, and from an extra judicial investigation it is clear that the interpellations would be practically impossible, hurtful or useless, then a dispensation from them may be obtained from Rome, and you will be declared free to marry a Catholic, presupposing, of course, that you are already one yourself."

"Well, Father," she said in quivering tones, "I won't annoy you any further with my marriage case." After fumbling about in her chatelaine she drew forth a water-stained clip-

ping. It was a brief account of poor Paxton's tragic demise.
"I suppose you saw this?" she asked.

"Oh, yes," replied the priest. "I was in Chicago when it happened."

"His death," she continued, "has not altered my purpose of entering the church. I shall never marry again and am really in a quandary just what to do. There seem to be only two vocations for women — either marry or enter a convent. Nobody has respect for an old maid."

"Where did you get those absurd notions?" asked Fr. Michaels. "Certainly not from Mrs. Grebma, because she knows better."

"No," replied Miss Seymour, "I have not broached the subject to her."

"Well," said Fr. Michaels, "I cannot account for the false idea entertained by even some Catholics, that single blessedness in the world is inferior to the marriage state. Long before the establishment of religious orders St. Paul declared: 'He that giveth his virgin in marriage doeth well, and he that giveth her not doeth better.' According to the Council of Trent, 'if anyone says that it is not a better and more blessed thing to remain in virginity or celibacy than to be joined in marriage, let him be anathema.' We Catholics believe that marriage is good, virginity or celibacy in the world better, and in the convent or monastery best of all. A woman in the world not bound by vows may be individually more perfect than a cloistered nun, if she loves God more, but the nun is in a more perfect state. The convent, with its enclosure, regular prayers and other spiritual exercises, implies to a greater extent than in the world the absence of temptation and makes detachment permanent — these two conditions which usually insure the perfect love of God. Considering the married state, celibate life in the world or in the convent as to individuals, the order of comparison may be reversed. Matrimony is the vocation of the majority, and in the language of the Apostle, 'it is a great sacrament; but I speak in Christ and in the Church.' St. Paul evidently alludes to Catholic and not mixed marriages. For those lacking a divine call religious life would be the worst state imaginable."

"What do you understand by a vocation, Father?" asked Miss Seymour.

"Vocation," replied Fr. Michaels, "is derived from *vocare* to call. It is a summons or call to some particular state or profession enabling one to preserve grace here, and to obtain everlasting happiness hereafter. The vocations of organized Christian society are the following three: the secular, ecclesiastical and religious. The first is based on the observance of the commandments; the second on the divine prerogatives of the priesthood and clerical duties; the third on the observance of the evangelical counsels. 'Everyone hath his proper gift from God; one after this manner and another after that. As the Lord hath distributed to everyone, as God hath called everyone so let him walk. He gave some (to be) apostles, and some prophets, and other some evangelists, and other some pastors and doctors, for the perfecting of the saints, for the work of the ministry, for the building up of the body of Christ.' God who has established by His providence the diversity of employments, distributes them differently by His wisdom. He designs some for one occupation and some for another. Hence He endows men with different inclinations and natural abilities, corporal as well as spiritual. He also distributes amongst them His graces diversely according to their respective needs. We all should follow that vocation which we sincerely believe to be most conformable to God's will and for which He has endowed us with the most aptitude and inclination."

"And supposing we don't follow our vocation?" demanded Miss Seymour.

"To neglect one's vocation," replied Fr. Michaels, "strictly speaking does not imply any sin whatever, for counsels impose no obligation. In this they radically differ from precepts. Yet the person neglecting to follow his vocation is hardly free from some fault on account of the danger to which he exposes his eternal salvation. He would not be free from grievous sin should he neglect to embrace the religious life, if firmly convinced that it was the only means of saving his soul. According to St. Liguori, persons morally certain of their religious vocation, yet who would fain persuade themselves that they can reach heaven just as easily in a secular pursuit, run great risk. They deprive themselves of many graces which God would have given them in the state to which He called them. Hence they encounter greater difficulties in resisting temptation."

"What are the signs of a religious vocation?" asked Miss Seymour.

"Oh, natural fitness for religious life in general, and a special liking for the rule and discipline of some religious community in particular," responded Fr. Michaels. "The candidate for religious life must not be fond of dazzling jewelry or gorgeous raiment, since she makes a vow of poverty. Her heart must not be longing for the ballroom, theater parties, receptions, joy rides and like amusements which would be incompatible with her vow of chastity. She must not be anxious to have her own way, but be gifted with an agreeable, submissive disposition, because by her vow of obedience she surrenders what we cling to most tenaciously — the sense of being our own master. Finally she must be drawn to the convent by proper motives, as e. g. because it seems to her the easiest way of being saved, God's glory, or the salvation of others. It is always best to consult some prudent and disinterested person in a matter of so great importance."

"Do you think that any convent would take me?" anxiously demanded the young lady.

"The House of the Good Shepherd," replied Fr. Michaels, "would certainly accept you upon my recommendation. If you wish, I will give you a letter of introduction to the Mother Superior. For the present, your vocation is to learn the catechism thoroughly and pray that God may make known to you His will. After you have spent a few months in the religious atmosphere of the convent and have become a member of the Church, you can seek advice from your spiritual director. He will assist you in deciding what path in life God wishes you to follow."

THE END